VEDIC DEITIES

M.P. PANDIT

PUBLISHER:
LOTUS LIGHT PUBLICATIONS
P.O. Box 2
Wilmot, WI 53192 U.S.A.

FIRST U.S. EDITION AUGUST 15, 1989

Published by Lotus Light Publications
by arrangement with Sri M.P. Pandit

ISBN: 0-941524-45-0

Library of Congress Catalog Card Number 89-084765

Printed in the United States of America

PREFACE

These studies seek to bring out the spiritual character of the Veda applying Sri Aurobindo's method of Esoteric Interpretation. Are the God's of the Veda Nature-elements deified by a primitive society or are they essentially divine Powers and Personalities of a Supreme Godhead? And if they are these, what precisely is their significance in the life of the Rishi of the Vedic age, or for that matter — since spiritual verities are of perpetual moment — to the Truth-seeker of Today? These are the main questions dealt with in the book.

The Deities chosen, Aditi, Surya and the Maruts, are among those that have not received adequate attention from the modern scholars so far. Besides, these are the ones that are most summarily dismissed as obviously personified natural phenomena. This is an approach to arrive at the full truth of their nature on the basis of the Hymns in which they have been celebrated by the Seers.

The studies closely follow the guidance and the writings of Sri Kapali Sastriar, especially his monumental Commentary on the First Asktaka of the Rig Veda, *Siddhanjana.* For his constant help and lead my gratitude is eternal.

M.P. Pandit

CONTENTS

TO

SRI KAPALI SASTRIAR

गङ्गायास्तीर्थमादाय
तस्यां तस्यै जलाञ्जलि :

ADITI

MOTHER WORSHIP OF THE MYSTICS

AMONG the Gods and Goddesses of the Rig Veda, Aditi is an outstanding figure of the Godhead, and her preeminence is arresting and rich with features as we shall see in this dissertation. She does not easily lend herself to classification among Nature-powers with the result that most of the western scholars have been admittedly baffled in fixing her identity. There is a fair measure of agreement among them that this deity represents a personification of some impersonality that pervades the physical universe. In working out this clue, some of them have indeed stumbled upon the fringe of what appears to be her true nature, but they have stopped short and refrained from further pursuit lest, perhaps, they may be led to findings which might upset the apple-cart of conclusions of their scientifically learned investigations. We propose to proceed from where they have left, with the necessary alterations, and arrive at a fuller truth, as far as is possible to gather from the Vedas themselves.

Scholars like Oldenburg would have it that Aditi is a personification of the idea of freedom from bondage. Explaining etymologically, they point out that the root *dī* signifies to cut, to limit, and hence, *aditi*, its privative, means that which is not limited, not bound. Muir goes on to develop this idea of boundlessness and states: "Aditi an ancient God or Goddess, is in reality the earliest name invented to express the Infinite; not he hastens to add, the Infinite", "as the result of a long process of abstract reasoning, but the visible Infinite, the endless expanse beyond the earth, the clouds, beyond the sky." Max Muller too is satisfied that Aditi is simply the 'infinite expanse visible to the naked eye.' Roth goes a step further and writes that Aditi, the mother of the Gods, Adityas, "eternity or the eternal, is the element which sustains them (Adityas) and is sustained by them... the eternal and the inviolable element in which the Adityas dwell and which forms their essence, is the celestial light...the Adityas, the Gods of this light, do not therefore by any means coincide with any of the forms in which light is manifested in the universe. They are neither sun nor moon, nor stars nor dawn, but the eternal sustainers of this luminous life which exists, as it were, behind all these phenomena." To this scholar, Aditi signifies in other contexts, imperishableness and also the boundlessness of heaven. We need not take note here of the hazardous verdict of scholars of Wilson's generation to whom Aditi is "evidently allegorical". We have only to observe the note of consistency among these scholars generally ascribing a character of impersonality of this Deity. She is an abstract concept or at the best an impersonal Power. There are, undoubtedly, Mantras which support this reading. But there are also so many utterances in the Vedas which address Aditi as a personal Deity, a Deity with as vivid and real an individuality as Agni, Indra and others. The Rishis invoke her and speak of their approach to her and the response they receive in terms which can apply only to a Deity who is as personal and real as any other God of the theist. There is thus a seeming contradiction and one is at a loss to know the the real character and function of this Deity. Is she a personal or an impersonal Deity? What is the function she is charged with in the cosmogony of the Vedic conception? If we follow the line of studying the Vedas vouchsafed to us by Sri Aurobindo, the difficulty is resolved and we arrive at a more adequate and completer understanding of Aditi, who is described as the motherliest of the Gods, *mātṛtamā*, an epithet obviously out of place for an abstract idea or conceptual form of the Indeterminate such as Aditi is made to be.

II

It is generally believed that Mother-worship in India owes its origin to the Tantric cults which developed long after the passing of the eras of the Veda and the Upanishad. But this is an error. Mother-worship finds a significant place in the religions of all ancient civilisations —including the Vedic—and this ought to be no surprise. For, man has found all along that of all relationships that of the mother and child is the purest, most sublime, natural and attractive. In this relation the usual barriers and human considerations of self-interest are transcended and the gates are opened on wider vistas where beat the wings of the Love Divine. And what could be more natural for the awakened human soul than to conceive of the Lord of all creation in terms of this parental relation? God was thus adored as the Father, as the Mother. In ancient Persia, for instance, it was as Father that the Creator was approached, while in many other societies, it was as the Mother. Thus were worshipped Isis in Egypt, Ashtart in Phoenicia, Demeter in Greece, Cybele 'The Mother of the Gods' in Rome. The Vedic pantheon contains a number of celebrated Goddesses, each looked upon as the fount of a particular line of manifestation in the cosmos. Embracing and containing all these Goddesses and the Gods,[1] the matrix from which all have taken birth, stands Aditi, widely expanded,[2]

[1] *viśvadrvyāvati* (Shukla Yajur Veda, II. 61)

[2] *uruvyacā* (Rv. V. 46. 6)

coextensive with all that is manifest, supporter of all.[1] She is the Infinite Consciousness of the Supreme in extension for the purpose of bringing forth from the Unmanifest what is to be manifested, for upbearing and sustaining what is thus released into the play of becoming. It is in this vastness of Consciousness that all disappear at the end of the journey; enveloping all, overtopping all, She it is who devours, *ad* to swallow, *atti*, *aditi*.[2] "We see in the Veda that Aditi, the Mother of the Gods, is described both as the Cow and as the general Mother; she is the Supreme Light and all radiances proceed from her. Psychologically, Aditi is the supreme or infinite Consciousness, mother of the gods, in opposition to Danu or Diti, the divided consciousness, mother of Vritra and the other Danavas—enemies of the gods and of man in his progress. In a more general aspect she is the source of all the cosmic forms of consciousness from the physical upwards." (*Sri Aurobindo*) But she is not that alone, nor merely Consciousness. She is, in the vision and realisation of the seers of the Veda, a great Deity, *mahi*, individualised and active in the exercise of her cosmic functions. She is a Divine Personality of whom other God-personalities like Indra, Agni, Varuna are the offsprings. From her they take birth; these God-powers are brought into manifestation only after the creation has been made possible by the outsurge of the active Consciousness of the Supreme, by the advent of Aditi. With her as the background and support they act and move. That is why in many of the Riks we see Aditi addressed *as* Varuna, *as* Agni, etc. Not merely the Gods,

---

[1] *dhārayat kṣitim* (Rv. I. 136. 3)

[2] Naturally, in this study we follow the derivation given by Sri Aurobindo who observes: 'Not that the word Aditi is etymologically the privative of Diti; the two words derive from entirely different roots, *ad* and *di*'. (*On the Veda*)

but everything in creation is thus dependent on Aditi, the Great Mother. It is thus that Rishi Gotama invokes her:

Aditi is heaven, Aditi is the region of mid-air, Aditi is the Mother, she is the Father, she is the son. Aditi is all the Gods, Aditi is the peoples of fivefold birth, Aditi is all that is born, Aditi is all that is to be born.[1]

Aditi is the heaven. In the symbolism of the Vedic mystics, the heaven stands for the higher consciousness of the pure mind which tops this lower creation. Aditi is that consciousness which is objectively extended as the plane or world known by that name in the universe, and in the individual subjectively manifest on his higher mental summits. She is also the *antarikṣa*, the mid-region, that is to say, the consciousness that governs and also spreads itself on a level of Being where the dominant principle is life-force, the breath of life, *vāyu*. Thus Aditi is both the heaven of mind and the mid-world of life-force in the graded levels of creation. This truth applies as much to the inner as to the objective existence. Aditi is the Mother, the matrix from which all springs forth, she is the material cause of all creation, of her substance is everything formed. Even the most physical things are what they are and live to be because they are instinct with this Consciousness. She is also the active cause, the Father of creation. This is so because this Consciousness is not a separate Power or Principle which the supreme Creator handles, but is itself the inalienable nature of

---

[1] *aditir dyau raditirantarikṣamaditir mātā sa pitā sa putraḥ |*

viśve devā aditih panca jana aditir jātamaditir janitvam ||

(Rv. I. 89. 10)

The English renderings of Mantras, in this study, are from Sri T. V. Kapali Sastriar's translations.

his Being. In this sense she is he. Again, the seer points out, she is the son; it is she herself, this boundless Consciousness, that assumes the bounded form of the many. She is not simply above and transcendent as the Father of the creation, nor is she only at the back of it, sustaining it with her motherly substance; she issues forth as the creation itself, the son that is born. She is the *viśve devāḥ*, All the Gods. All the deities of the Veda are powers and personalities, emanations put forth from the supreme Creator for purposes of manifestation out of his own Being whose nature is Consciousness that is Aditi. It is thus that the Gods are said to be born of Aditi, to be Aditi herself. So is Usha described as a front of Aditi.[1] It is this truth that finds expression in the utterance of the later sages of the Upanishad, *aditir devatāmayī*.

She is the *pañca janāḥ*. Commentators have generally taken this expression to signify the five kinds of beings, viz. Gandharvas, Fathers, Gods, Asuras and Rakshasas or the five orders of men, Brahmana, Kshatriya, Vaishya, Shudra and the Nishada to make up the fifth. But the matter does not seem to be so simple. Sri Kapali Sastriar draws attention, in his Rig Veda Bhashya, to the variety of views in olden times on the question and cites a passage from the Brihad Devata in witness:

"Some say the five peoples are the Five Fires—Shalamukhya, Pranita, Son of Grihapati, the Northern and the Southern Agnis; others say they are Men, Fathers, Gods, Gandharvas, Uraga-Rakshasas, or following Yaska, they are Gandharvas, Fathers, Gods, Asuras, Yaksha-Rakshasas. Shakatayana thinks they are four Varnas and the fifth the Nishada. Shakapuni says they are the Ritviks (officiating priests) five in number—Hota, Adhvaryu,

---

1. *aditeranīkam* (Rv. I. 113·19)

Udgata, Brahma and the Sacrificer, Yajamana. But the Atmavadins (who are for the inner meaning of the Veda) hold that they are the Sight, the Audience, the Mind, the Voice and the Life. The Aitareya Brahmana speaks of Gandharva-Apsaras, Gods, Men,—Fathers and Serpents. Other Yajnikas refer to other creatures of the earth and the Gods. (Br. D. VII. 67·12)"[1]

In the esoteric evaluation of the symbols used by the Rishis, it would rather appear that *pañca janāḥ* signifies those of fivefold birth, who are born five times. In their system of cosmology, the entire creation is conceived in five rising tiers, viz. earth, sky, heaven, Mahas, the world of Light, and then the upper half, *parārdha*; and man, the epitome of this creation, contains in himself, subjectively, the different principles governing these five different orders of the creation and lives simultaneously on these five levels of his being. Thus he is born and lives at the same time on the physical, the vital, the mental, and—whether he is aware of it or not in his external consciousness—on the super-mental and still higher planes. Thus is man of 'fivefold birth.' And they too, these beings, says the Rishi, are Aditi, because it is this Consciousness that constitutes the stuff of their existence on the several levels of their being. These five planes themselves, be it remembered, are the varied formations of this one manifested Consciousness, varied to suit the manifold purpose of the Supreme's Becoming.

The Rishi has till now described Aditi in so many significant expressions, affirmed her in terms of one now and then another. Why continue this endless enumeration, he seems to feel, and with that naturalness which always characterises the Vedic seers in giving expression, in a few

[1]Rig Veda Bhashya (Introduction).

simple words, to the most staggering and over-whelming conceptions (and realisations), he declares: She is all that is born and She is also all that is to be born. That is indeed the essence of the matter. Modern scholars have drawn attention to a happy parallel found among Egyptian Inscriptions. In one of the temples of Goddess Neith, the Great Mother, in the city of Sais, is found inscribed in Greek:

Ego: eimi pan to gegonos kai on kai esomenon kai ton emon peplon audeis po: thne: tos apekalupsen.

"I am all that is and that was and that shall be, and no mortal hath lifted my veil."

This magnificence in her impersonality, however, is not the whole truth of this mighty Deity. She is a personality that is accessible to the Gods in heaven and to men on earth. She takes an active part in the governance of the cosmos. It is of her that another seer sings:

May we call to Aditi for protection, who is, verily, the great builder of those who are engaged in happy works, who is the Consort of Truth, whose strength is manifold; who never ages, who embraces the Vast, who is a happy shelter, who is perfect in her leading.[1]

Aditi is not only the Mother from whom all take birth. She is a builder, not indeed of everything in the general sense—that is already implied in her motherhood—but specially of those who are devoted to auspicious works. Such ones, whether they be Gods or men, are shaped by her. To the Vedic mystics, the *suvrata*, happy,

---

[1] *mahīm ū ṣu mātaram suvratānām ṛtasya patnim avase huvema,* |

tuvikṣatrām acaratim urucim suśarmanam aditim supranitam ||

(Yajur Veda, 21. 5; Atharva, VII. 6. 2)

auspicious work, in the case of man is the sacrifice, self-giving, the inner discipline by which he learns to consecrate progressively his life to the call of the Higher Truth; while in the case of the Gods, *suvrata*, happy, auspicious work, is a happy discharge of the functions with which they are entrusted in the cosmic manifestation viz. to help and lead the human soul onward on the path to the higher Felicity, to keep the wheels of creation moving on the lines of the Truth, the Right, the Vast, *satyam ṛtam bṛhat*. Of such, says the Rishi, Aditi is the great builder; she builds greatly unlike the many other powers and energies which are active in contributing to the growth of man, each in its own definite and fixed direction. She enables them to withstand the arduous demands of the Work they are engaged in, she endows them with strength to develop greater and yet greater capacities, she moulds them into an increasing perfection which images something of her own wholeness.

She is *ṛtasya patnī*. Ritam, in the thought-system of the Vedic seers, is Satyam, Truth, in manifestation. Ritam is the status of the Divine Truth turned towards manifestation, its way of workings, the Right, the Law that ultimately governs and lends meaning to the Creation. All exists for that Truth: Earth and Heaven, wide and deep, are there for the Rita, the Truth, for the Truth's working'.[1] Its foundations are fixed firmly,[2] the highest Gods are its guardians, *ṛtasya gopāḥ*. The Gods are what they are because they are *ṛtāvanā*, possessed of the Truth.[3] Rita manifests the Godhead: 'The Truth's directives increase me (in might and substance)', says Indra address-

---

[1] *ṛtasya pṛthvi bahule gabhire* (Rv. IV. 23. 10)

[2] *ṛtasya dṛlhā dharuṇāni santi* (Rv. IV. 23. 9)

[3] Rv. VIII. 25. I.

ing the Rishi Nema.[1] Indeed, it is identified, by some seers, with the Divinity itself.[2] And as the consort of Ritam, Aditi is inalienable from it; where Ritam is, there is Aditi. Again, in the Vedic, as in all Eastern traditions, the wife, the female principle stands for the power of effectuation, the Shakti of later ages, and in this sense Aditi is the power and means of manifestation of Rita who is her Lord. Aditi is thus indispensable to bring forth into the foreground and release into operation the potencies that lie in the concentrated content of Ritam.

To play this many-sided role, to contain, to bear and conduct this multi-hued and many-tiered creation, she needs must have a *manifold* strength. Her power, her might takes different shapes and expressions appropriate to the levels on which it is to function. And taken as a whole, her strength is thus active simultaneously in a manifold way. She does not age. Herself the fount of all life and energy, Aditi cannot flag; She is not subject to the operations of Time which after all is one die in her game, thrown at her will. She is eternally young and fresh. If she is thus unlimited by Time, she is not limited by Space either. She is coextensive with the Vast in whose hollow the many universes appear and disappear. Embracing all, she provides succour, support, a shelter that not merely protects but promotes happiness. She is, says the seer, masterly in leading. Those who consecrate, equip and put themselves in the hands of this Mighty Mother receive her lead and help consciously and speedily; the rest too are led by her, but without their conscious cooperation. In either case, her workings are

---

[1] *ṛtasya mā pradiṣo vardhayanti.*

[2] *hamsaḥ...ṛtam bṛhat.*

skilfully tempered to meet the need and nature of every individual; they anticipate and provide for every contingency with a far-seeing eye. And where does she lead?

May we ascend Aditi for Beatitude, the Divine ship endowed with quick propellers, faultless, intact without slits, a capable protector, spacious as earth, like heaven to which no hurt can come, a happy shelter and skilful carrier.[1]

To Beatitude, declares the Rishi. From evil and suffering, incapacity and decay, that characterise normal mortal life, Aditi, the Mother, leads her children to joy and strength, to Bliss which is ultimately the goal and the true, intimate nature of Creation. Normally human beings are limited severely in the ego-dominated islets of consciouness and hence miss the true nature and significance of life. As they grow and develop in the ways of the *suvrata*, they learn to break or outleap these barriers and allow themselves to partake of the joy and delight which come naturally to a being freed, unbounded in consciousness. To launch on this journey of pilgrimage, the seer invokes the aid of Aditi whom he compares to a ship. She is the divine vessel that navigates the waters of existence, waters interspersed with liberal scatterings of the shoals and rocks of ignorance and falsehood, desires and passions and their brood in the ego-bound life. Here is an image, be it noted, that recurs frequently in later spiritual literature, the figure of the boat which at one time or other, in the life of the seeker, ceases to be a mere symbol and answers to a fact of spiritual experience. (Cf. *Durg¯si durga-bhavasāgara-naurasangā*, Thou art

---

[1] *sutrāmānam pṛthivīm dyāmanehasam suśarmāṇamaditim
ṣupraṇitam* |
Daivīm nāvam svaritrāmanāgasamsravantīmā ruhema svastaye ||
(Shukla Yajur Veda, 21. 6)

not accessible with ease, Thou who art without attachment, art the raft to cross the hard seas of life.)

The expanse to be covered is vast and this divine ship is specially endowed with propellers that speed her across with needed quickness; there is no halt or tarrying for him who ascends this ship. She is faultless in her working and impregnable in her construction. There are no defective chinks in her armour through which the treacherous Enemy can strike. The breakers from the rough seas may strike and strike but the ship moves on intact. Thus is she a capable protector of those who deliver themselves to her charge. There is no end to her bounty; for she is as spacious as the earth itself. In a sense, we may add, this ship is carrying the whole earth towards its destination. Her arms are extended to all who turn to her. She offers the security and the felicity of heaven where the missiles of the nether creation reach not. To such a unique ship, the seer repeats, let us aspire.

Let me ascend for blessedness the auspicious ship intact without a rift, without fault, endowed with a hundred propellers.[1]

Note how he repeats the epithets to emphasise their significance, as if to warn all in his hearing not to be misled in boarding other pseudo-ships which are plentiful in this world of ignorance and falsehood, ships that are found to have dangerous slits, faulty operation, when it is too late. This ship, he says, is auspicious, it is auspicious because all who have set their feet on its board have been moved and inspired by one auspicious Will, the very body of the carrier is of the stuff of auspiciousness itself and the destination of the journey on which it has set out is the most auspicious, the

---

[1] *sunāvamāruheyamasravantīmanāgasam* |
ṡatāritrā svastaye || (Shukla Yajurveda 21. 7)

Highest Beatitude. The ship has a hundred propellers. In the Vedic parlance figures of ten, hundred, thousand signify graded completeness, a rounded fullness. The ship is equipped with, the seer purports to say, a full complement of power and speed which is total and adequate for the purpose of completing the voyage to the other shore of blessedness; the blessedness or beatitude to which she leads is not merely freedom from bondage and suffering, it is a positive condition in which the being is gifted by her with the manifold treasure of the Spirit. Listen to another seer:

For plenitude's delivery we call by the Word, verily, the great Mother Aditi, she in whose lap is the wide mid-world, let her grant us a happy shelter of three abodes (or three bars).[1]

Vaja is usually taken to mean, by Sayana, food, though at times other meanings are given, e.g., cattle, speed, strength, etc. In the psychological interpretation, *vaja*, according to Sri Aurobindo, uniformly signifies plenitude, *samṛddhi* plenty, of whatever it may be, of strength or food or something else. Aditi holds in herself the Powers of Abundance, capacities to enlarge, increase and fill to overflow the wealth that is prayed for, whether material or spiritual. In the context, naturally, it is the prosperity of the spiritual character that is sought after. Divine Knowledge, Power, Bliss, these are the treasures which enrich the soul, mind and life, they are the plenty that do not decay. It is in the gift of Aditi to shower them in abundance on those whom she chooses. Human effort alone cannot win them. She has

---

[1] *vājasya nu prasave mahimaditim nāma vacasā karāmahe |*

yāsyā upastha urvantarikṣam sā naḥ śarma trivarutham ni yacchāt || (Atharva Veda VII. 6. 4)

to bring them out of her depths and deliver to the recipient who has sufficiently purified and prepared himself to hold and retain these godly possessions. For such a gift the Rishi with his comrades invokes the Great Mother. They wait upon her with the Word of call which is the one unfailing means for the Vedic Mystic to reach the Gods.

The *Word*, we must remember, has a special significance in the Veda. To give an adequate idea of what it means to the Rishis, we cannot do better than quote from the relevant writings of Sri Aurobindo:

"In the system of the Mystics, which has partially survived in the schools of Indian Yoga, the Word is a power, the Word creates. For all creation is expression, everything exists already in the secret abode of the Infinite, *guhā hitam*, and has only to be brought out here in apparent form by the active consciousness. Certain schools of Vedic thought even suppose the worlds to have been created by the goddess Word and sound as first etheric vibration to have preceded formation. In the Veda itself there are passages which treat the poetic measures of the sacred mantras,—*anuṣtubh*, *triṣtubh*; *jagati*, *gāyatri*,—as symbolic rhythms in which the universal movement of things is cast.

"By expression then we create and men are even said to create the gods in themselves by the Mantra. Again, that which we have created in our consciousness by the Word, we can fix there by the Word to become part of ourselves and effective not only in our inner life but upon the outer physical world. By expression we form, by affirmation we establish. As a power of expression the word is termed *gih* or *vacas*; as a power of affirmation, *stoma*...Fashioned by the heart, it receives its just place in the mentality through confirmation by the mind. The Mantra, though it expresses thought in mind, is not in its essential part a creation of the intellect. To be the sacred and effective word, it must have come as an inspiration from the supramental plane, termed in Veda, Ritam, the Truth, and have been received into the superficial consciousness either through the heart or by the luminous intelligence, *manīṣā* ... it is ... by the power of the heart that the Mantra takes form. But it has to be received and held in the thought of the intelligence as well as in the perceptions of the heart; for not till the intelligence has accepted and even brooded upon it, can that truth of thought which the truth of the Word expresses be firmly possessed nor normally effective." (*On the Veda*)

Or, to cite another passage:

"The theory of the Mantra is that it is a word of power born out of the secret depths of our being where it has been brooded upon by a deeper consciousness than the mental, framed in the heart and not constructed by the intellect, held in the mind, again concentrated on by the waking mental consciousness and then thrown out silently or vocally—the silent word is perhaps held to be more potent than the spoken—precisely for the work of creation. The Mantra can not only create new subjective states in ourselves, alter our psychical being, reveal knowledge and faculties we did not before possess, can not only produce similar results in other minds than that of the user, but can produce vibrations in the mental and vital atmosphere which result in effects, in actions and even in the production of material forms on the physical plane." (*Kena Upaniṣad*)

This is the Word, emerging out of the inner being of the Rishi in the heat of Tapas, the sound-form of a truth which has been realised in the soul-depths, the Word which is therefore alive with a spiritual power to reach its destination, that is employed by them to invoke the Goddess.

The Great Mother, she who contains the inexhaustible plenitudes in her own being, is so vast in her spread that the entire mid-world spanning the oceanic spaces between the Heavens above and the Earth below is held in her lap. There lies the source of all the mighty life-forces and energies that constitute the warp and woof of the mid-world. May she, concludes the seer, grant us the happy shelter of the three abodes (or three bars).

He asks for a three-storeyed or three-barred abode. The normal life of man is led on three levels, that of the body, the life-force, *prāṇa*, and the mind. They are the three concurrent statuses of his existence. The Rishi seeks protection on each of these three fronts, individually, because the nature of the dangers to which he is exposed is different on each level. The body, for instance, is constantly threatened by the forces of disease, decay and death; the *prāṇa*, life-force, is in danger of being maimed or mis-directed by the beings of the vital world; the mind is an ever-inviting prey to the thousand and one trappings of ignorance and falsehood. The shelter of Aditi provides protection against all these enemies as it is triple-tiered in its guard.

We have so far seen some of the epithets which the Rishis have used to describe her personality, her bounty. There are some more which are to be noted. In a hymn to the All-Gods, Vishve Devah, Vasishtha calls upon them—Mitra, Varuna and Aditi, for deliverance from trouble. And here are his three appellations for Aditi which deserve mention for their significance:

...*Aditi, easy to call, luminous, immobile (or horseless)*...[1]

She is *suhavā*, easy to call, i.e., she gives ready response to our call. Now if Aditi were simply a name for Infinity or an Impersonality, this epithet could hardly make sense. Only a personality, a being, can take note of and respond to a call. The epithet emphasises that one can communicate with her, have relations with her; she is in this sense personal, a personality. She is *devi*, luminous (or divine), not a mere etheric extension without form; her form is lustrous because Light is the robe of pure Consciousness that is natural to her being. She is *anarvā*, immobile or as Sayana takes it, unassailed; or it could mean, without horse, vehicle. *Arva* means horse; Aditi is horseless, i.e., she does not require a vehicle to move with as she is the All and the Mother of the Gods, the Infinite, present wherever the call reaches. All the Gods in the Veda, as we know, have their own vehicles which, as Sri Kapali Sastriar points out, are 'symbolical, intimately expressive of the truth and character of the Gods visible to the inner vision of the Rishis.' He cites Yaska's mention of the vehicles of Indra, Agni, and other Gods. "Indra has two green horses, Agni's ruddy, Aditya's tawny, Ashwins have two donkeys and Pushan goats; antelopes of Maruts, rosy rays of Ushas and Savitr's dusky horses along with the vehicle of Brihaspati called Vishwarupa are mentioned and Vayu's horses are called Niyuta."[2]

But Aditi has no vehicle, because she has no need for one, she, indeed, being present everywhere in her mighty extension as the Infinite being, Or it is plausible to take it as unassailable, *apratigatā*, as Sayana does.

---

[1] *suhavā Dėvyāditiranarvā* (Rv. VII 40. 4)

[2] *Further Lights : The Veda and the Tantra*

In another Rik addressed to Mitra and Varuna, Rishi Puruchhepa prays that the ever-wakeful two Gods may arrive and be present

"...*in union with Aditi who is full of splendour, who is in possession of the world of Truth-Light, who is the upholder of the peoples.*"[1]

She is *jyotismatī*, full of splendour, because it is in her that the light of the divine Consciousness in manifestation is focussed, marshalled and thence radiated in different directions. She is *svarvatī*, one who holds the world of *svar*, the Truth-Light, the world which overtops this lower creation of ours and forms the link between the Upper Half, *parārdha*—the worlds of Sat, Chit and Ananda, and the lower half, *aparārdha*, constituted by our worlds of matter, life and mind. This intermediate world is governed by the Divine Truth whose form is Light; that is why it is known also as Mahas. In a sense it is the source or starting-point of creation. Here is what Sri Aurobindo calls the Real-Idea, the original truth of things in seed-form, the final poise of the One before he gets abroad as the Many; it is a status and therefore a natural possession of Aditi, the supreme creatrix of All. She upholds the *peoples*. Not merely men living on earth, but the inhabitants of all the worlds in creation draw the wherewithal of their existence from Her.

A Rik of Seer Jamadagni is even more significant:

Mother of Maruts (Rudra's sons), Daughter of Vasus, Aditya's sister, navel-centre of Immortality, the Ray-Cow, Aditi,

---

[1] *jyotiṣmatīmaditim dhārayatkṣitim svarvatīm*

(Rv. 1. 136. 3)

the faultless, 'Hurt her not'. This I declare to the people who have understanding.[1]

The Rudras, the progeny or the hosts of Rudra, the God who brooks no obstacle, are the Maruts born of Prishni, *pṛsni-mātaraḥ* (Rv. I. 23. 10), Prishni being the dappled Cow which symbolises Aditi of the mid-region. The Maruts, the storm-gods in the external sense, are "thought-powers energised by the radiances of Indra the God of the Divine Mind, but being primarily born of the Life-Force, they are also the nourishers of the nerve-forces...their mother is the cow of variegated hue which means symbolically the Shakti who is the field for the manifestation of the Life-power, who contains in her womb the rays of thought-power, who fills the mid-region with her infinite extension as Aditi, endowed with capacities for bringing out diverse manifestations, the multi-hued Cow, Prishni, the mother of Maruts."[2]

The Vasus in the Veda are the Dwellers in substance; they are the divine Powers who exist for the great Substance, the Earth, which is indeed fashioned and looked after by these mighty guardians. And Aditi in her status on the physical plane, identified with the Earth comes to be described as the daughter of the Vasus. The Adityas are the Gods that abide on the higher, the supra-terrestrial planes; of them she is the sister. In the Veda, the term *svasr* is used to denote constant association, *sāhacarya*. Aditi, the Great Goddess, is so closely associated with these Powers of creation that the seer describes her as their

---

[1] *mātā rudrāṇām duhitā vasūnām svasādityānāmamrtasya nābhiḥ |*

pra nu vocam cikituṣe janāya mā gāmanāgāmaditim vadhiṣṭa | (Rv. VIII. 101. 15)

[2] Sri Kapali Sastriar: *Rig Veda Bhāśya*

sister. Thus we have in this Rik description of Aditi in her different status on the three planes of Existence. She is again the navel-centre, the nodus of immortality. As the Infinite Consciousness of the Supreme Being, she is the nerve-centre at the core, the fountain-spring of that immortality which pervades at its roots the entire creation. That is so because immortality is the very nature of that Being. The more one grows into her Consciousness, the nearer one gets to this *amṛta* and all that issues from it. To widen into the ampler reaches of the infinity that is Aditi is to break out of the barriers of death and sorrow and partake increasingly of the bracing zephyr of immortality that ever breathes out from her.

She is the Cow, not indeed the physical quadruped which is the outer form and symbol, but the Cow of Light. In Sanskrit, *go* means at once the cow and the ray. This *double entendre* of the word led the Rishis to treat the physical cow as a symbol of light. And when they speak of the Consciousness of the Supreme Being, as Light, this image of the cow comes with a happy naturalness. "In the ancient Indian system of thought being and consciousness were aspects of each other, and Aditi, infinite existence from whom the gods are born, described as the Mother with her seven names and seven seats (*dhāmāni*), is also conceived as the infinite consciousness, the Cow, the primal Light manifest in seven Radiances, *sapta gāvaḥ*" (Sri Aurobindo: *On the Veda*), She is the *faultless* cow, faultless because in the very nature of things this intense and gapless Consciousness whose content is the Truth, the Right, could hardly have any blemish. She is, another seer describes her, *aghnyā*,[1] the Cow that cannot be slain—'the Infinite Mother—the supreme

---

[1] *aghnyāyāḥ dhenoḥ* (Rv. IV. I. 6)

Divine Consciousness creative of the Cosmos, of the gods and the demons, of men and of all that is.'[1] "Hurt her not", the Rishi imperatively calls and declares that he speaks only to those who have understanding. In the context, it is clear, the cow could hardly be the bovine quadruped inasmuch as one does not need to be specially gifted with understanding to listen to this call. The Rishi addresses those who are awakened, whose mind is open to the higher Consciousness, to so conduct themselves, to so live their life that nothing they do runs contrary to the pristine vibrations of this Mother of Light, nothing jars and hurts on her universal, extended Being. Continuing his exhortation, the Rishi delivers one of the most pregnant utterances in the whole of the Rig Veda. He speaks out of the fullness of his inner realisation; he clothes in sound-form the truth granted to his hearing by Aditi herself. Aditi declares:

Small-minded mortal avoids me, the Ray-Cow, Goddess come for the sake of the Gods, who brings with her voice uplifted, who is present close by with (illumined) thoughts.[2]

As a rule, man is limited to the confines of his sense-bound physical mind. He does not exert himself to broaden and heighten the reach of his mental regions and as a result, he is captive in the hold of limitation, incapacity and all that constitutes mortality. He even tends to avoid all that would disturb his smug security. The hold of tamas, obscurity and inconscience is so great that man hugs his little life of ignorance refusing, under

---

[1] Sri Aurobindo

[2] *vacovidam vācamudīrayantīm viśvābhirdhibhirupatiṣṭhamā nām* |
devīm devebhyaḥ paryeyuṣīm gāmā māvṛkta martyo dabhracetāḥ ||

one plea or another, to be wafted by the liberating breath of the Spirit that ever flows from above. Aditi the Cow of the Infinite Consciousness as Light is thus shunned by the mortal man whose lot it is to shut himself in the obscure dungeon of his physical mind. The ego-bound personality of man is afraid of getting lost and merged in the infinitude of Knowledge if it were to come face to face with this Dynamo of Light of Knowledge.

She is come for the sake of the Gods; the Gods, who are personalities and powers put out from the Divine Being to secure, conduct and promote the cosmic manifestation; they could not fulfil their function but for the all-pervading and sustaining presence of Aditi. Children of hers, they lean on her—the "navel-centre of immortality"—for nourishment; as the Cow of Light, she provides all the fund of knowledge and illumination that is required by the Gods. She brings the creative Word, Word the sound-substance of power, that dynamites the rocks and mountains of Inconscience and Ignorance and opens the Gates of release for the aspiring forces in creation. To the mystics of the Veda, engaged in lifelong Tapasya, nothing is more indispensable than the Word—the Mantra—which blasts the obstacles and barriers that defy all human effort to break them. Aditi brings the Word in an unmistakable manner; she announces it loudly with a clarion voice. She is, concludes the Rik, present, close to us, if we will, with her treasure of illumined thoughts. She is the reservoir of knowledge, of illumined thought-currents that flow from it constantly enriching the Fund of Knowledge at the disposal of man emerging out of the nether seas of sheer physicality. She is accessible, as close as we choose, ready to shower the gifts on those who turn to her. To Her, says seer Brihaduktha.

Let us pile well the sacred grass; let Aditi be pleased with it (the seat) which is wide, spacious and spread over the Earth, with the Gods upon it; and with a common pleasure with the Gods, bestowing delight uphold it in the auspicious abode.[1]

Let us arrange the seat kept ready for Her. "The sacred grass, *barhiḥ*, is the symbol used in the ritual to prepare the seat. It is to be spread (*stīrṇa*) in due form... well prepared...the seat is indeed within the inner being of man. It must not be supposed that it is a point of some imagined spot or the heart in the physical frame of the human being. The seat for the Gods is indeed within, in the inner being which is wider and far greater and subtler and supple and enlightened and distinguished from the physical being. We have to speak of it as within, because the outer self and the outgoing mind and vital activities are all but a modicum of that larger being behind and even encompassing them. Once the initiation into the secret path that leads to the inner chamber takes effect, the outer normal self of man with all its thinkings and doings dwindles into a nothing before the wideness at the threshold of the Vast Self within in which the sacred seat of the Gods is arranged for the welcome of the Higher Powers."[2] The altar must be such that the Goddess is pleased with it; it must be so charged with the ardour of aspiration that it is irresistibly inviting. The seat must be wide, spread over the Earth, adds the seer significantly. That is, the inner being and consciousness must be so enlarged and universalised in scope as to

---

[1] *stīrṇam barhiḥ suṣṭarīmā juṣāṇorū pṛthu prathamānam pṛthivyām* |
devebhiryuktamaditiḥ sajoṣāḥ syonam kṛṇvānā suvitte dadhātu || (Shukla Yajurveda 29.4)

[2] Sri Kapali Sastriar: *Further Lights: The Veda & the Tantra*

embrace the whole earth. The Gods who are invitees for this *yajna* which is the path of inner sacrifice, must have arrived and taken their due places on the altar. That is, the various energies and powers on the different levels of the being must have attained their fulfilment and each occupying its rightful place set the altar in a harmonious whole. And when Aditi arrives to take her place on the altar, finding it in such a state of completeness, she, says the Rishi, will be pleased with it, and sharing her felicity with the hosts of the Gods present, each partaking his share, she will pour Delight, her immortal bliss on the altar, make it fit to ascend and live on the yet higher altitudes of the Spirit and establish it finally in the auspicious abode of Felicity which is the Goal of life's journey.

We thus see in these and similar Mantras the utmost reverence in which Goddess Aditi is held and worshipped by the Rishis of old. In the pantheon of the Vedic Gods, each God has his own Shakti, e.g. Agni has Agnayi, Indra Indrani, Varuna Varunani; but there are goddesses like Bharati, Sarasvati, Ila, who are worshipped in their own right. However, of all the Goddesses, as the Mother of all the Gods, Aditi enjoys a position which is solitary in its grandeur. She is the most notable example of a Diety in whom the Impersonal and the Personal fuse contrary, perhaps, to all canons of reason and logic, but naturally and self-evidently to the spiritual vision and realisation of the seers. She has many aspects in which her Personality manifests itself though her transcendence and release from all Names and Forms is never lost to view in her mighty Impersonality on which the stress falls not seldom in the hymns of these mystics of ancient wisdom. And it is to the credit of the Tantriks of a later age that they preserved and developed the truth of these aspects of Her as the different lines of Shakti at work, e.g. Adya Shakti, Transcendent Mother, Para Shakti, Supreme Mother, Maha Shakti, Mother of of the Cosmos and their further sub-divisions which is a different matter and a vast subject beyond the scope of this study. The hymns we have illustrated should serve to draw attention to the dominant role the Mother-worship played in that age, a fact which needs to be pointed out and stressed in view of the theory, advanced by some of the modern scholars, that Mother-worship was unknown among the Vedic Aryans and came to be borrowed from alien civilisations like the Dravidian. The Divine Mother is invoked and worshipped by these seers in many forms. No doubt in the later Vedantic age, the stress is more and more completely shifted to the Purusha and the Goddess slides into the background even as in the still later developments of the Tantric age, the Shakti comes to predominate relegating the Purusha into a passive poise in practice. But the fact remains that the Supreme Mother is held in the highest esteem by the Rishis of the Veda and adored as Aditi with the same fervour and devotion as charcterises their approach to the other Gods of the ancient Pantheon.

SURYA

THE VEDIC SUN

Among the prayers of invocation bequeathed by the Rishis of the Vedic past a pre-eminent place is taken by the great Mantra of Savitr, well-known after the metre in which it is cast—*Gayatri*; the verse reads:

> *Tat savitur vareṇyaṁ bhargo devasya dhīmahi dhiyo yo naḥ pracodayāt*,

or, in English,

> We meditate upon that excellent splendour of the God Savitr.
>
> May He impel our thoughts.

For countless generations in India this Rik of Rishi Vishwamitra[1] is being repeated with an unquestioned faith in the sacred character of the origin and certainty of its efficacy. And yet, to a casual reader, the lines contain nothing beyond a pious wish that one's thoughts may be impelled by the sun in the sky. The sun is indeed known to have certain properties to promote life in plants and vegetables, the rays are even known to have certain therapeutic virtues for the cure of bodily ills; but nowhere do we have it that there is any connection between the human mind and the solar orb in the sky. How then to account for this call to the sun to actuate the movements of the mind? Could it be simply a survival of what many modern scholars have been content to describe as

---

[1] Rig Veda, III. 62. 10

Unless otherwise mentioned, all the English renderings of Riks in this study are from Sri T. V. Kapali Sastriar's translations.

superstitious beliefs of the Hindus in that primitive stage which characterises all early human societies, when animism, nature-worship and anthropomorphism play a dominating role in shaping the lives of men? In that case the prayer would be nothing more than a formal chanting of supplication to a power of Nature and could not hope to claim the allegiance of thinking minds even thousands of years after it was handed down by the Rishis. But it is a fact that even the most inveterate sceptic, when he comes to this verse of Gayatri, cannot help feeling that here there must be something more than what at first meets the eye. To understand the secret of its hold on the Indian mind it is necessary to know something of the character of the lives and aspirations of the Seers to whom the Mantra owes its parentage.

Let us state at once that we do not accept the position that these Fathers of the Aryan race, the Rishis of the Veda, are simple bards of an unsophisticated age given to glorify Nature-powers in order to ward off their supposed wrath and win their benevolence in favour of the supplicants. The Rishis are the leaders of a people that lived and prospered in an age in which truths of spiritual character had as much, if not more, immediacy of appeal and relevancy as facts of physical Nature. It was an age when religion played an intimate part in the lives of men, albeit with varying emphasis depending upon the level of refinement of the classes. The Rishis represent the vanguard of this civilisation and contain in themselves the essence of the spiritual effort and achievement of their society. To the Vedic Rishi life has a double aspect, the outer and the inner. The outer external life of himself and of the universe around is supported by and governed to a more or less extent by the inner. The outer derives its full meaning and significance by the inner of which it is a figure and living symbol. The real purpose of life is achieved on the inner reaches of the being and then transmitted to the outer. And what is the purpose that was sought to be achieved? It is to grow out of the falsehood, ignorance, crookedness and mortality into the ampler sweeps of spiritual Truth, Knowledge, the Right, the Immortality. The whole endeavour is imaged as a journey which is effected with the constant help and guidance of the Gods who are conceived and realised as so many emanations from the Supreme[1] put forward to maintain and govern the cosmos in manifestation. The Vedic Gods also are thus endowed with a double aspect; one the external, as powers presiding over the main activities of Nature and the other the inner, psychological, the Powers that manifest and build up the Truths of Knowledge, Dynamis, Beatitude etc. Thus Indra, the Lord of the Gods, is in his external aspect the Deity who heads the storm-gods, causes life-giving waters to rain and generally uses his irresistible thunderbolt to smash the enemy of his subjects. But that is not all. To the Rishi, to the traveller on the Mystic Path, Indra is the God who presides over the Divine Mind, that summit of the Mind where the human is transcended and the reign of the pure Heavens is begun. In close parallel to his outer function, Indra heads the thought-powers, causes streams of pure creative energies to outpour on the furrowed expanses of the aspiring being and uses his rod of light—the thunderbolt of Knowledge—to dissipate and

---

[1] *viśve devā aditiḥ* (Rv. I. 89. 10)

sarve hyasmin devatā gāvo goṣtha ivāsate (Av. II. 8. 32).

sarve asmin devā ekavṛto bhavanti (Av. 13. 4.21).

yo devānām nāmadhā eka eva (Rv. X. 82. 3)

break down all clouds of darkness and inertia. Similarly Agni, the Mouth of the Gods, besides being the deity presiding over the third element in Nature, is the God who takes birth as the flame of aspiration, grows up as enlightened Will in action and leads the sacrificer on, with himself remaining in the front, *puro hita*. The full import of the utterances of the Rishis, the real nature and character of the Gods whom the seers invoke and adore, the true significance of the fruits of their worship and sacrifice, come to be appreciated only when we recognise that here is a record of a mighty spiritual endeavour, a chart of huge expanses of the Spirit traversed and mapped out, a touching epic song preserving for all time the melodies of home-coming of the Aryan Soul to the Divine Creator.

It is in this setting that the God invoked in the Gayatri verse is to be looked at and the meaning of the invocation understood. Like the other Gods in the Vedic pantheon, the Sun, Surya, also signifies more than what he seems in his outer aspect viz. the solar deity radiating heat and light. "The Sun, Savitr, is not the physical sun we see in the skies, but the supreme Effulgence in the highest firmament above, beyond the lower triple creation. The physical sun is indeed taken as the image of the Truth-Sun, the Centre of all Knowledge and radiating Power. It is the radiance issuing from the Supreme Source in which is massed all the creative movement of the Uncreate that is the ultimate root of all movements in the creation. Let that Light motivate and energise our thought-movements, says the Rishi."[1]

---

[1] Sri T. V. Kapali Sastriar : *Further Lights* : *the Veda and the Tantra.*

II

It is a fact of spiritual experience that Light is the vesture in which Spiritual Truth reveals itself. The supreme Truth, no doubt, is beyond all form. Still when it manifests itself it takes the form of Light. Even the physical light that we see around carries within itself the truth of a spiritual Force that dispels ignorance and gloom and bakes the being in the illuminating light of Knowledge. That is why the universal forces of ignorance and falsehood, disease and death are more pronounced in their sway during the night when light is not and that is also why the opposite forces of creative knowledge, happiness and life find themselves quickened and active during the day.[1] Light indicates the presence of a Truth of which it is an awakening symbol. The Sun itself is, as Sri Aurobindo has pointed out, "the symbol of concentrated light of Truth." "Do not imagine that light is created by the Suns. The Suns are only physical concentrations of Light, but the splendour they concentrate for us is self-born and everywhere. God is every where and wherever God is, there is Light, *jñānaṁ caitanyaṁ jyotir Brahma*". (Sri Aurobindo)

To the Vedic Mystics this was a self-evident truth[2]

---

[1] *Vide* Essays on the Gita (2nd series, Chap. III): "Yogic experience shows in fact that there is a real psycho-physical truth, not indeed absolute in its application, behind this idea, viz. that in the inner struggle between the powers of the Light and the powers of the Darkness, the former tend to have a natural prevalence in the bright periods of the day or the year, the latter in the dark periods, and this balance may last until the fundamental victory is won." (Sri Aurobindo)

[2] *agneranīkam bṛhataḥ saparyām divi śukram yajatam sūryasya* (Rv. X. 7. 3)

I honour as the face of lofty Agni in heaven the bright and holy light of Surya. (Tr. by Griffiths)

and in their system of symbolism in which they translated and preserved their account of inner realisations on the God-Path, the physical sun was the symbol or representative of the Sun of Spiritual Truth who stood at the head of Creation. All life's journey of the Rishi was directed towards the eventual attainment of this supreme Source and presiding Deity of all that is manifest.[1] Towards this glorious end they sought the help and support of other Gods to whom they offered the best in themselves and whom they invoked in so many inspired hymns of praise. Practical men that they were, they occupied themselves consistently with the means whereby to reach their Goal of the Highest Truth-Sun above the firmaments of the worlds and did not lose time in ideation about the nature of the Reality, the Person of this highest God. That is why we find in the Rig Veda many more hymns are devoted to Gods like Indra, Agni and others with whom the Rishis were in constant immediate relation and whose help was most urgent for their progress and only a few to Surya though he was the target of their adventure. This fact has misled many western scholars in declaring that Surya is a 'minor deity' in the Veda. That leads us to the confusion of understanding in which these scholars have landed themselves in their approach to the Gods of the Veda. We shall here concern ourselves only with the subject at hand, viz. Surya in the Vedic hymns.

If to the western scholars and men of their way of thinking, Surya in the Veda is nothing more than the solar orb whom Nature-worshipping Aryans lauded as a god or perhaps an occult entity or power imagined by them to be presiding over this phenomenon in Nature, it

---

[1] *ātmā jagatastasthuṣaśca* (Rv. I. 115. 1)

is because they have approached the subject with preconceived ideas formed by their studies of societies elsewhere and sought to find data to tally with their notions of what the early Aryan societies in India must have been. Things would be assuredly different if they came with an open mind and saw clearly what the Rishis themselves have to say about the Gods. To that we will turn later. It is a record of history that the Sun has played an important part in the development of religion in many of the early civilisations in Asia and elsewhere, notably in the Egyptian, the Mayan, the Babylonean and the Japanese. In Egypt the Sun-God Aton 'represented by a disk with rays extended as benevolent hands' came to be the benign Deity of a highly ethical religion, while in Mexico, the Sun was pictured as a Jaguar to whom human sacrifice was dear. Thus solar worship was to be found among many peoples and the aforesaid scholars saw the Vedic Surya as but one more parallel. If the Sun-God in Egypt was conceived as a child at daybreak, *Horus of the East*, as a hero in the mid-day, *Ra*, as old man in the evening, *Temu*, the Sun in India also must undergo the same transmogrification. He is Surya in the day, Savita during the night and so on. Besides, the descriptions of the Sun, as indeed of other gods, are done in such a close-knit parallelism of language by the Rishis, that the same epithets can apply to the deities as conceived in the external form by the common man as well as they can to the god-heads in their inner and psychological aspect. The descriptions of Surya are the most deceptive in this regard. In the case of Indra, or in the case of Agni, there are many epithets which are wholly inapplicable to them in their exterior form as rain-god and the elemental fire-god. But with Surya, within the limited number of hymns, the incongruity is not so easily striking. But the fact remains that Surya addressed in these hymns is not merely the physical sun; he is much more; he is 'the divine being in his creative and illuminative solar form'. (Sri Aurobindo) We will now cite some specimens of the relevant Riks and passages from the Rig Veda and show how they substantiate this position of the esoteric interpretation of the Veda.

Here is a Rik describing the journey to the Sun.

Beholding the loftier light that springs up above Darkness we have come to the Sun, the God among Gods, the most excellent (loftiest) light.[1]

The Rishi declares that he and his companions in *tapasyā* have arrived at the Sun. How did they arrive? They beheld the lofty light and followed its lead. And what is this light they speak of? It is the light that has sprung up above, *ut*, the *tamas*, the darkness; it is leading still upwards *uttaram*, and culminates in the supreme Effulgence, *uttamaṁ jyotiḥ*. The graded ascent from height to height is to be noted. Following this growing Light the Rishis have attained *aganma*, the Sun. Commenting upon this Rik, Sayana himself says that as an alternative, the *tamas* means *sin*, and drawing on the Brahmanas in support, says *pāpmā eva* etc.; and explaining the term *aganma*, points out that the Rishis attained union with the Sun, *ādityasya sāyujyaṁ gacchati*...Now clearly this Sun whose light is beyond *sin* and with whom the Tapaswins attain conscious union cannot be the physical sun. That is why even scholars like Wilson are constrained to note: "Here again we may have an allusion to a spiritual sun. The darkness, it is said, implies sin, and the

---

[1] *udvayam tamasaspari jyotispasyanta uttaram |*
devam devatrā sūryamaganma jyotiruttamam || (Rv. I. 50. 10)

approach to the Sun intimates re-union with the supreme spirit." The purport of this Rik is self-evident. In the course of their spiritual effort the seekers have glimpsed the light of the Sun of Spiritual Truth; at first it is just above the grey murk of ignorance and dense physicality in which the world is wrapped. They behold it and, beholding, follow it up in its expanding emergence till it gradually joins with its parent-source, the loftiest, the transcendent Luminary of Spiritual Truth, the Surya who is resplendently outstanding naturally in the bright assembly of the Gods, *devaṁ devatrā*. He is the most excellent Light; in this the original station of the creative Light, there is yet no shadow to mar or lessen the perfection of its Splendour which exceeds the earthly splendour of a thousand suns[1].

I have known this great Being of Solar splendour and hue beyond Darkness. Having known him one goes beyond death; there is no path to the Goal other than this.[2]

The seer states he has *known* i.e. realised, the supreme Purusha whose appearance is that of the sun. Where is the Purusha whose likeness is the sun? He is beyond Darkness, *tamasaḥ parastāt*. Again, darkness here could hardly make meaning if it meant nothing more than the dark of the night. And what follows leaves us no doubt about the real meaning. For the Rishi goes on to add, to know the sun-like Purusha is to cross beyond death, i.e. to conquer mortality. That can be said, by no stretch of imagination, of the physical sun. To realise one's identity

---

[1] *divi sūryasahasrasya bhavet yugapadutthitā |*
yadi bhāḥ sadṛśi sā syād bhāsastasya mahātmanaḥ ||
(Gita XI. 12)

[2] *vedāhametam puruṣam mahāntamādityavarṇam tamasah parastāt |*
tameva viditvāti mṛtyumeti nānyaḥ panthā vidyati'yanāya ||
(Yajurveda 31. 18)

with this Being is to exceed one's human limitations, outgrow the tutelage of ignorance and pass beyond the rule of birth and death and attain immortality. To attain this immortality there is no other way except this, viz. to strive and attain the supreme Purusha whose form is that of the sun, *ādityavarṇaṁ*. Mark that the Purusha is not the *āditya* but One who is aditya-like. The sun we see in the sky is chosen to image his likeness; the sun is 'the physical form of Surya, Lord of Light and Truth; it is through the Truth that we arrive at Immortality, the final aim of the Vedic discipline'. (Sri Aurobindo)[1]

Of Savitr sing the glory, the offspring of Waters, for protection. We desire his laws.[2]

The Rishi describes the Sun as *apaṁ napatam.* Sayana explains it as *jalasya na pālakam*, one who does not protect or cherish the waters, meaning thereby one who scorches up the waters, *santāpena śoṣakam.* But the usual sense of the word *napāt* in the Veda is son, progeny. How can the Sun be said to be the son of Waters, is it not Agni who is consistently lauded as the child of waters, it may be asked. The Waters represent the universal creative energies out of which the worlds get fashioned, they are the inconscient waters, *apraketaṁ salilaṁ*, out of which creation flowers out and this creation, be it remembered, is a willed projection of the Lord of Truth of something of his own Substance,[3] a birth of himself in

---

[1] Though this verse is not in the Rig Veda, it is cited here for the wide currency it has acquired for hymnal purposes, specially whenever the Purusha Sukta is chanted.

[2] *apām napātamavase savitāramupastuhi |*
tasya vratānyuśmasi || (Rv. I. 22. 6)

[3] *puruṣa evedam sarvam yad bhūtam yaśca bhavyam |*
(Rv. X. 90. 2)

a special sense. In the individual, the Waters signify the streams of conscious energy, creative currents of light and power whose first child in man is Agni, the flame of aspiration, the will to achieve and progress. And once the onward progress of man is thus commenced impelled by Agni, the birth of the subsequent offspring, the vision of the spiritual Sun is the inevitable goal towards which all the movements of his life converge.[1] We thus see how naturally the epithet *apāṁ napātam* applies to Surya and there is no need to construe the word as Sayana has done. The absurdity of the usual gross explanation of Sun being the offspring of waters because he rises from the ocean every morning is too patent to be emphasised. Such explanations may have held water when geography was the handmaid of mythology but they stand out of court in our day.

Of such a One, Surya the child of the Waters, seek the protection, says the Rishi and goes on to add that they desire his Laws; he aspires, with his companions, to know and possess the ways of his working which are indeed faultless and self-fulfilling because they proceed from and are the natural modes in which the unclouded royal Sun of Truth manifests his glory. To apply these epithets to the sun in the sky would be simply puerile.

I call upon Savitr, golden-handed, for protection. He is the Cognisant, the Person who is all the Gods, the Goal for attainment.[2]

The seer invokes God Savitr for protection, *utaye*, which can also mean for increase—increase obviously of

---

[1] *Vide* Sri Kapali Sastriar: *Rig Veda Bhāṣya*

[2] *hiraṇyapāṇimūtaye savitāramupahvaye |*
sa cettā devatā padam || (Rv. I. 22. 5)

his spiritual stature. Savitr is 'golden-handed'. In many Riks Savitr is described as golden coloured in arms, hands, hair, face, etc. Modern scholars generally dismiss the epithet as a mere figure of speech and pass on. But the term must be significant particularly since it is repeated consistently in so mamy Riks. As Sri Aurobindo observes: "Gold is in the Veda probably the symbol of the substance of the truth, for its substance is the light which is the golden wealth found in Surya...".

He is the supreme Cognisant. As the universal Knower he indeed knows everything; but he is the cogniser in the individual also. It is as a result of his functioning, direct or indirect, that the consciousness that perceives is active in man. He is the Purusha who has become all the Gods.[1] All the other Gods derive their existence from Him; that is why they are said to follow his lead.[2] His is the picturesque Face of the Gods[3], He is the very Eye of Mitra, the God of Love and Harmony, of Varuna of Wideness and Purity, of Agni, the immortal among mortals.[4] He is also the Goal, the ultimate end to reach which all beings strive, knowingly or unknowingly. To Him as the supreme Creator all creation turns.[5]

Dweller in the Mighty, in the excellent, in the Truth, in the sky, born of waters, of Ray-Cows, of the Right, of the Hill, the Truth.[6]

---

[1] *ekam santam bahudhā kalpayanti* (Rv. X. 114. 5)

[2] *yasya prayāṇamanvanya idyayurdeva |*
devasya mahimānamojasā || (Rv. V. 81. 3)

[3] *citram devānām...anīkam* (Rv. I. 115. 1.)

[4] *cakṣurmitrasya varuṇasyāgneḥ* (Rv. I. 115. 1)

[5] *tam vartaniranu vāvṛata*

[6] *nṛṣad varasad ṛtasad vyomasad abjā gōja ṛtajā adrijā ṛtam.* (Rv. IV. 40. 5)

These are the descriptions of Surya by Vamadeva in the Rig Veda. The Sun—the Swan of the Heaven—dwells in his own Home where all is Might, all is of the highest order and that is so because it is the Truth itself. The highest plane which is the abode of the Spiritual Sun is the Plane of Truth, of Satya. He is in the *sky*, that is, he is spread out in his own extension. He is born of the Waters of creative conscious energies. He is born of Ray-Cows. The rays signify rays of illumination, of Knowledge, and the advent of these rays always precedes the emergence of the Sun in his plenary form; the Ray-Cows deliver the Sun as it were. He is born of Rita, Right, the Law of Truth. It is by growing into the Law of Truth, by making it the Law of one's own being, that the birth of the Sun of Knowledge in oneself is achieved.[1] He, the Sun, is born of the Hill and hill in the Veda, as we know, stands for Existence; the Sun takes birth and manifests in the being of the worshipper as a result of his *tapasya*. He is thus born on the many-tiered hill of the Yajamana's being. Surya is the Truth itself—the Truth-Sun at the head of Creation and above, greater than it.[2]

Do these epithets apply to the physical sun?

Another Rik is still more explicit. The Rishi calls upon his companions to chant to Indra, the superb slayer of Vritra, that mighty Saman by which

---

[1] To such a one who knows the Law, says, another seer, the very winds are sweet, the rivers pour sweet.

madhuvātā ṛtāyate madhu kṣaranti sindhavah (Rv. I. 90. 6)

[2] *ato jyāyānsca pūruṣaḥ* (Rv. X. 90. 3)

They who increase truth brought into birth the wakeful light, a god for the god.[1]

The Light is wakeful; it is living and conscious and keeps him, in whom it is active, awake to the higher call. It is brought into birth by them who are *ṛtāvṛdhaḥ*; *satya-vardhakaḥ*, Sayana puts it, those who open to the Divine Truth, aspire for its birth in them and by steady aspiration and discipline promote its all round growth in their being. In such men does the Light that is conscient take birth—god for god, the Sun of the Spiritual Truth is born to illuminate and vivify the God Indra, the Divine Mind.

If there be any doubt still left about the nature and origin of Surya hymned in the Veda, the following Rik of Rishi Vishwamitra leaves no ambiguity on the matter.

Where comrade with comrades, the Navagwas close by, followed seeking the Ray-Cows with bended knees, there Indra verily with ten Dashagwas discovered the Truth that is the Sun lying in the darkness.[2]

The allusion is to the legend of the Angirasas into the essentials of which it is but necessary for our purpose to enter. Suffice it to say that the Angirasas are the Flame-Powers of Agni active for the spiritual advancement of man and the manifestation of the Divine Truth. The question whether the Angirasas are Gods who have taken human form or originally Rishis who have been

---

[1] *yena jyotirajanayan ṛtāvṛdho devam devāya jāgṛvi*
(Rv. VIII. 89. 1)

[2] *sakhā ha yatra sakhibhirnavagvairabhijñā satvabhirgā anugman* |
satyam tadindro daśabhirdaśagvaiḥ sūryam viveda tamasi kṣiyantam || (Rv. III. 39. 5)

apotheosised need not detain us here. They are the helpers and comrades of Indra in his search for the Ray-Cows of Knowledge which are concealed in the dark caves of primeval Ignorance by the ancient Enemy. Indra sets out to free these Cows (of Illumination) for the benefit of his subjects, viz. humanity. The Navagwas and the Dashagwas are two different classes of Angirasas who join him in the hunt. The Power of the Divine Mind is closely associated and led by the flaming powers of Will and dynamism raised to white heat in the being of man in the struggle for the recovery of the saving light. They go on bended knees, not erect and free. For the ways to the nether regions of sub-conscience and falsehood are crooked, low and are fashioned in all cunning. The investing hosts have to accommodate themselves to these tortuous alleys. And at the end of their quest, Indra and his companions find the Sun *lying in darkness*. What is this Sun? He is, says the seer in unequivocal terms, the Truth as Sun, Truth in the form of the Sun. Sayana himself casting aside all his ritualistic preferences, states boldly, *satyaṁ, yathārthaprakāśaṁ, sūryaṁ*, the Sun that is the truth *tamasi kṣiyantaṁ andhaḥkāre nivasantam*, dwelling in the darkness. The Darkness, it goes without saying, is the darkness of Ignorance and Inconscience in which the precious light has been imprisoned by the Enemy and denied to man. This is the same Light which another Rishi speaks of[1] as the Light which Indra finds amid the blinding Darkness of dense Inconscience.

The Surya is constantly referred to in association with Horses. The Horses speed him to the end of the earth.

---

[1] *so andhe cit tamasi jyotirvidan* (Rv. I. 100. 8)

The seven coursers harnessed to thy chariot bear thee for ever, O Wide-seeing One, God Surya, bright-haired.[1]

The horses of Surya signify his Rays, his emanations that trail the path he is to traverse. They are described as seven in number, seven being the number of the cosmic principles of Creation of which He is the Lord. (Bhuh, Bhuvah, Svar, Maha, Jana, Tapah and Satyam are the seven world-principles underlying the manifestation.) These significant facts should not be lost sight of; the Rishis repeat time and again that the Sun's horses are seven. Some of the western scholars would have it that these seven horses are the seven days of the week. Does it follow that the Rishis of India had a calendar of seven-day week? But these very authorities teach us that the seven-day calendar originated among the Accadians, Babylonians and then Greeks!

Surya has yoked the pure-bright mares born of the Car; with them self-harnessed he goes forth.[2]

The seven shining mares are *born* of the car. Car, *ratha*, indicates movement and it is out of the expansive and pervasive movement of the Sun that his Rays of illumination proceed. Thus they are the outflowings of the Sun in the becoming; and they are self-harnessed. They continue, in the very nature of things, to be intimately connected with their parent-source for otherwise they can have no existence of their own.

The auspicious bright horses of Surya, of veriegated hue, who merit our pleasing laudation and traverse fast have mounted

---

[1] *sapta tvā harito rathe vahanti sūrya* |
śociṣkeśam vicakṣaṇa || (Rv. I. 50. 8)

[2] *Ayukta sapta śundhyuvaḥ sūro rathasya naptyaḥ* |
tābhiryāti svayuktibhiḥ || (Rv. I. 50. 9)

to the ridge of Heaven reverencing (their Master) and in an instant speed round Earth and Heaven.[1]

The Horses, i.e. Rays of the Sun bring felicity in their wake; hence they are auspicious; they are conscient *par excellence*, hence radiant; they are potent of endless qualities, so they are multi-hued; they travel fast as becomes the carriers of the All-Creator and instinct with fealty and adoration to their Master they appear on the summit of the Heavens of the Pure Mind of the Rishi. Such is their power that directly they appear on the tops of the pure mental heavens, they spread all over the Earth and Heaven, they enrobe in their light the entire physical being with the life and the mind of man.

Can these descriptions hold good in the case of the physical sun? As Sri Kapali Sastriar observes: "If it is the external sun, the horses would be first seen in the Eastern quarter, not on *divaḥ pṛṣṭhe*, the ridge of heaven".[2]

We have now known from where Surya rises, where he dwells, what are his bay horses. We shall now look into a few Riks for the workings of the Sun-God in the inner life of the Vedic Mystic.

Thou helpest to cross, Surya, all-beautiful, creator of lights, Thou illuminest all the radiant realm.[3]

He helps the seeker to cross the ocean of ignorance in which men are normally immersed or afloat. The

---

[1] *bhadrā aśvā haritaḥ sūryasya citrā etagvā anumādyāsaḥ | namasyanto diva ā pṛṣṭhamasthuḥ pari dyāvāpṛthivī yanti sadyaḥ* || (Rv. I. 115. 3)

[2] Rig Veda Bhashya

[3] *taraṇirviśvadarśato jyotiṣkṛd asi sūrya | viśvamābhāsi rocanam* || (Rv. I. 50. 4)

seeker has to get over what appear to be interminable tracts of darkness, inertia and obstruction in his own being before he can arrive at the threshold of the freer regions of the spirit. The rays of the Sun help him to surmount these obstacles. He is the creator of lights that light up his path, flood the obscure regions with revealing light. All lights within and without are derived from this supreme Creator of lights, *tameva bhāntam anubhāti sarvam.*[1] All the spaces above the belt of ignorance are illumined by the rays of the Sun. Once the mystic traveller crosses the shore of darkness, *tamasaspāram*, the warmth and splendour of the radiance issuing from the Truth-Sun is a self-revealed fact to which all spiritual history bears constant testimony. It is interesting to note that after commenting on this Rik in the usual naturalistic sense, Sayana goes on to give what Wilson calls 'metaphysical explanation'; he identifies "the sun with the supreme spirit who enables all beings to cross over the ocean of existence, who is beheld by all desirous of final emancipation, who is the author of true or spiritual light and who renders everything luminous through the light of the mind."[2]

God of Vast felicity who brings into being and causes to rest what moves and what moves not; he who has control over both.

---

[1] Katha Upanishad ; Mundaka Upanishad.

[2] *yadvā ye sūrya antaryāmitayā sarvasya prerakaḥ paramātman taraniḥ samṣārābdheḥ tārakosi yasmāttvam viśvadarśatah viśvaih sarvairmumukṣubhirdarśato draṣṭavyaḥ sāksāt kartavya ityarthaḥ...jyotiṣkrt jyotiṣaḥ sūryādeh kartā...īdrśastvam cidrūpatayā viśvam sarvam dṛśyajātam rocanam rocamānam dīpyamānam yathā bhavati tathā ābhāsi prakāśayasi caitanyasphurane hi sarvam jagad drśyate* (*sayana*).

May he, the God Savitr, grant us shelter with triple abode (or bar) against evil."[1]

Surya is the showerer of happiness for which, unlike the human joys, there is no limit; the felicity he radiates on those who seek him is boundless. As the supreme Creator it is he who is responsible for the manifestation or withdrawal from manifestation of all that is.[2] Mobile or immobile, every part in creation is under the control of Savitr. The Rishi prays to such a one for shelter. Shelter against whom? against the Evil, the misery and distress that stare on all sides in this world threatening to overwhelm any one who dares to win the Good, the Beatific and the Joyous. He asks that the protection, the bar, must be *triple*. It must be effective on all the three levels of his being which are every moment exposed to danger, viz. his body, his life, his mind. Savitr can grant him this protection because there is no end to his bounty, not a whit beyond his control.

Can the physical sun be imagined to vouchsafe this triple guard?

Surya pursues the refulgent Dawn as a man of vigour (follows) a lovely maiden, where men spread the sacrifice for ages towards the Auspicious One for the Auspicious.[3]

---

[1] *bṛhatsumnaḥ prasavitā niveśano jagataḥ sthāturubhayasya yo vaśi* |

sa no devaḥ savitā śarma yacchatvasme kṣayāya trivarūthamamhasaḥ || (Rv. IV. 53. 6)

[2] *yaḥ parthivāni rajāmsi vimame* (Rv. V. 81. 3)

[3] *suryo devimuṣasam rochamānam maryo na yoṣamabhyeti paścāt* |

yatra naro devayantho yugāni vitanvati prati bhadrāya bhadram || (Rv. I. 115. 2)

The Sun of Truth does not reveal himself all of a sudden to the worshipper. Before the advent of the Sun there is the outbreak of the dawn which intervenes between the Night from which the *tapasvin* is emerging and the Day he aspires to enter. This Dawn of the Divine Consciousness is the precursor of the rise of the Sun on the horizon of the topmost being of man. But the Dawn and then the rise of the Sun cannot be continuous because of the inability of the seeker to hold the Light uninterrupted in himself. The system has to be trained to respond to the demands of this Consciousness and needs periods of assimilation and preparation during which the Light withdraws behind the veil. That is the meaning of the several dawns which are followed inevitably by the effulgent Sun. Note it is the Divine Dawn, *devim usasam*, which is pursued or followed after by the Sun who is compared to a man of vigour, *marya*, not a weakling, but a full-blooded youth, to emphasise the strength and power of the Divine Truth that is manifesting. And in the wake of this Dawn, the worshippers spread the sacrifice *for ages*, for the attainment of the Auspicious. How can a sacrifice be spread *for ages* during the brief period of the physical dawn? The incongruity disappears only when we read the passage in the light of the inner context; it is the divine Dawn of Consciousness that is referred to. The duration of this Dawn varies from individual to individual but it is certainly not short. It is long enough and lasts till the seeker perfects his sacrifice and is fully prepared to emerge into the ever-lasting Day.

The same truth of the withdrawal of the Light at intervals in order to let the being assimilate what it has received and to prepare itself for more is repeated in the following Rik.

Such is the Godhead, such the might of Surya. He withdraws what is spread over unfinished work.

The Sun is the supreme Master; he floods with his lustre when he pleases, he withdraws his rays when he chooses. In the midst of the work of perfecting the worshipper, the Yajamana, the Sun withdraws leaving the task apparently unfinished. Really, he waits for the moment when he can spread his rays still more effectively.

Radiant with kindly light, rising today, mounting to the loftier heaven, O Surya, dispel my heart's disease and the body's yellow hue.[2]

The light of the Sun is always kindly, agreeable, beneficial to him who is privileged to bask in its radiance. When the Sun mounts to the vaster heaven, *bṛhad-dyauḥ*, the wide firmament of the pure mental skies, his rays are specially potent and dynamic. And it is for these rays that the Rishi aspires; they are to cure him of the restlessness and want of peace which underlie all disorder of the mainspring of the system as also of all physical ailments. The yellow hue of the body results from the unhealthy condition of the blood and so here signifies disease of the body in general. Commenting on this Rik, Sri Kapali Sastriar notes:

Health, outer and inner, is to be obtained by the gift of the Surya who is traversing the lofty heavens. The seers of the Mantras hold that some kind of *siddhi*,

---

[1] *tatsūryasya devatvam tanmahitvam madhyā kartorvitatam sam jabhāra* |
yadidayukta haritaḥ sadhastādādrātri vāsastanute simasmai || **(Rv. I. 115. 4)**

[2] *udyannadya mitramaha ārohannuttarām divam* |
hṛdrogam mama sūrya harimāṇam ca nāśaya || **(Rv. I. 50.11)**

perfection, of the body also is indispensable. For the physical body becomes the pedestal of the God-aspiring man. That is why the Rishis wait upon the Gods with hymns such as 'let us with well-set bodies live the life in God's bounty,' 'may we live as heroes for a hundred springs,' etc."[1]

Grant us sight unto the eye, grant sight unto the bodies that they may see; may we thus see (all) this intimate and wide.[2]

Here again the Rishi prays to Surya for the weal of the body. He asks for the gift of sight to the eye; obviously it is not the physical sight alone for which this Jnanin prays to the Supreme God; he prays for the divine vision to which there is nothing unseen, nothing unseeable, nothing distant, the sight which is an undeflected truth-sight. He prays that his body also may be endowed with this eye; the body too must learn to *see*, i.e. to be fully conscious, vigilant against all that is malevolent and receptive to whatever uplifts. The Rishi prays that the body may be endowed with capacity to function in the right way with a spontaneously accurate response, without the need of guidance from the other members of the being.

Surya has spread his form as light: hither there came from far above the Mother of the Ray-Cows. The rivers flow to the deserts having swallowed the banks; and Heaven is firmly fixed like a pillar strongly set.[3]

---

[1] Rig Veda Bhashya

[2] *cakṣhurno dehi cakṣuṣe cakṣurvikhyai tanūbhyaḥ |*
sam cedam vi ca paśyema || (Rv. X. 158. 4)

[3] *vi sūryo amatim na śriyam sādorvādgavām mātā jānati gāt |*
dhanvarṇaso nadyaḥ khādo arṇāh sthūṇeva sumitā dṛmhata dyauḥ || (Rv. 45. 2)

From far above, that is from the heights of the spiritual being, from beyond the levels of the mind, the Dawn, parent of the rays of illumination, has arrived; the harbinger of the fuller light to follow comes first. Then rises the lustrous Surya giving his splendour not in diffused but in concrete form (*rūpamiva dravyam*, says Sayana.) The presence and light of the Surya make themselves felt in a very palpable manner. Certain definite results ensue. The streams of the superconscient forces invade the being of the worshipper, they inundate, they eat up the long established barriers of inertia, *tamas*, and obstinate habits of the body, the preferences and revolts of the life-being, the limiting constructions of the petty mind and its reasoning, barriers long settled in him against the free flow of the higher light and force. Overflowing these banks, they flow on to the desert regions of the rest of his being which are dry, parched up for the reason that they have not known the fertilising waters of the enlivening consciousness so long.

And the Heaven is established firmly. The worshipper has the heaven of the divine mind fully opened up on the summit of his being. It is firmly set; no external or internal movement can disturb this edifice; this pure consciousness is rendered active in its own right.

Surya mounts to the resplendent Waters where he yokes the wide-backed shining horses. The wise carry him like a ship through waters ; the waters giving their assent slowed down.[1]

The Sun of Truth ascends to the Waters. The Waters are the superconscient Ocean above the triple

---

[1] *ā sūryo aruhat śukramarno'yukta yaddharito vītapṛsṭhāh* |
udnā na navamanayanta dhīrā āśaṇvatīrāpo arvāgatisṭhan ||
(Rv. V. 45 10)

world of ignorance; they are resplendent because they are the energies of Consciousness treated to a high degree of Truth-Light. When the Sun finds his position above the Waters, he brings into action his radiant ray-powers which are wide-backed, capable of bearing the large charge of his Substance. The seeker in whom the Sun is manifested has to pass through the rapid-coursing Waters of the conscious energies and emerge out of them on the serenities of the unveiled Spirit. He has to hold to the Light and carry the Light that is revealed to him through the various levels of the graded existence where countless currents of Consciousness-energy are at flow; only the wise, *dhīrāḥ*, can navigate successfully these Waters like experienced ship-men. Narrating this, the Rishi recalls that when he carried the Sun in this manner the Waters cooperated with him in his high endeavour and ceased to be rash and obeyed so as not to upset his mission.

The Dark goes down restrained. The Rays of golden hue, robed in Waters, fly upwards to the Heaven. When they come down from the Home of Truth, the Earth is well worn with their clarity.[1]

In this beautiful Rik is contained one of the capital consummating realisations of spiritual life. With the steady advance of the pilgrim of Light under the benign guidance of the Gods, the darkness which has stamped itself as the inalienable shadow of human existence begins to lose its hold. Its grip loosens and step by step, under the relentless chase of the onsetting rays of the Sun it recedes gradually. These rays of golden hue are charged

[1] *kṛṣṇam myānam harayaḥ suparṇā apo vasānā divamutpatanti |*
ta āvavṛtrantsadanādṛtasyādid ghṛtena pṛthivi vyudyate ||
(Rv. I. 164. 47)

with the vibrations of the streams of consciousness as Energy of the higher planes, clothed in them, as it were, and because of this character they are able to shoot up from the heights of his being to the still loftier altitudes of the Home of the Truth, the Purest Heavens where Truth dwells in its full sway. And when the Rays come down from these heavens they are naturally charged with the consciousness proper to those summits and they pour all the light and knowledge with which they are loaded into the physical being of the blessed worshipper. The Earth is indeed spread over with the clarities of Rays fresh from Heaven.

We cannot help noting here what a parody of this sublime verse has been perpetrated by the gross and naturalistic interpretations. We are told that when the darkness of the night settles down, the sun's rays descend to the earth, absorb the moisture, rise again to the skies and then descend in the form of rain. Evidently the primitive bards of Vedic days were pretty good students only of Natural Geography!

Thus the Vedic lines here cited are but a few specimens—for instances can be multiplied to show the true character of the Sun in the Rig Veda. This, then, is Savitr the Creator, Surya the Impeller, the Sublime and Ultimate Truth represented by the sun in the physical universe formally, as the glorious figure and revealing Symbol for worship; but in reality the Sun that arises, in the words of Sri Aurobindo, 'is the Sun of the superconscient Truth; the day he brings is the day of the true life in the true knowledge, the night he dispels is the night of the ignorance which yet conceals the dawn in its bosom.'

THE MARUTS (I)

It is not very difficult to determine the psychological and spiritual character of Vedic deities like Agni, Surya, Soma, because there are unmistakable hints, transparent images and, in many places, direct expressions in the hymns which leave no doubt about the intention of the Seers. But what of the Gods whose nature and functionings are spoken in terms that are obviously physical? Where do we place the Maruts whose form and activities are uniformly described, in very many of the hymns, in their most physical character?

Children of Rudra, the God of wrath, and Prishni the dappled Cow, the Maruts, we learn, are hosts of the sky, moving ceaselessly in companies. They roar in thunder and flash like tongues of fire. They have axes of gold and spears of lightning. Their steeds are many-hued. They smite and smash what comes in their way, they pour down torrents of waters. Heaven and earth quake at their advent. With the wheels of their chariots they rend the mountain rocks. They are companions to Indra, the Lord of heaven, who releases the rains after Vritra the Adversary is struck down with their aid. They have a common place of birth; they all grow together on earth, in air and heaven and are of one mind; they rise from the ocean and pour the pail of heaven. They are self-luminous. They dispel darkness and lay the path for the sun.

In the context of the naturalistic interpretation, the similarity of these descriptions in the hymns with the external phenomena of storms have led to the identification of Maruts with the storm-winds that rage to the accompaniment of lightning and thunder. They are the gods of the tornado, the cyclone. They are personifications of these elemental forces that sweep the skies, tear out the trees and churn the water of the seas. This is the verdict of western scholars which is supported by the Ritualists. No doubt there are some differences of opinion among these scholars on grounds of etymology.[1] There is Benefy, for instance, for whom the Maruts are personifications of the souls of the dead from *mar*, *mṛ* to die. Max Muller derives the word from *mṛ* to pound, to smash, to destroy. But these do not affect the conclusions of modern scholars in any fundamental manner. To them, they are powers of storm in Nature, deified, as is usual with the ancient peoples of all countries, as gods and worshipped and propitiated as such, the Storm-gods. The Maruts of the Vedic Aryans and the Mars of the Greeks are to them identical. To quote Max Muller: "There can be no doubt about the meaning of the name, whatever difference of opinion there may be about its etymology. *Marut* and *maruta* in ordinary Sanskrit mean

---

[1] Among Indian commentators also, there has been a good deal of speculation about the derivation of *marut*. Sayana gives as many as four alternatives: *mitam nirmitam antharikṣam prāpya ruvanti* they sound (*ruvanti* from *ru*) having attained mid-heaved (*mitam*); *amitam bhṛśam śabdakāriṇaḥ* they sound without measure (*amitam*); *mitam swarnirmitam megham prāpya vidyudātmanā rocamānāḥ* | they shine (from *ruc*) with this lightning in the clouds made (*mitam*) by themselves; *mahati antharikṣe dravanti* they hasten (*dravanti*) in the sky. Yaska explains: *maruto mitarāvino vā* who sound measuredly, *mitarocino vā* or who shine with measure, *mahat dravanti vā* or who run very much. Durgacharya points out that some read the passage as *marutó mitarāviṇo vā amitarocino vā mah ravanti vā* which gives quite the contrary meaning, viz. they who sound without measure or in varied ways; they who shine limitlessly or in diverse hues; they who roar loudly.

wind, and more particularly a strong wind, differing by its violent character from *vāyu* or *vāta*. Nor do the hymns themselves leave us in any doubt as to the natural phenomena with which the Maruts are identified. Storms which root up the trees of the forest, lightning, thunder, and showers of rain, are the background from which the Maruts in their personal and dramatic character rise before our eyes. In one verse the Maruts are the very phenomena of nature convulsed by a thunderstorm; in the next, with the slightest change of expression, they are young men, driving on chariots, hurling the thunderbolt, and crushing the clouds in order to win the rain. Now they are the sons of Rudra and Prishni, the friends and brothers of Indra, now they quarrel with Indra and claim their own rightful share of praise and sacrifice. Nay, after a time the storm-gods in India, like the storm-gods in other countries, obtain a kind of supremacy, and are invoked by themselves, as if there were no other gods beside them...We can observe the transition of the gods of storms into the gods of destruction and war, not only in the Veda but likewise in the mythology of the Polynesians; and yet the similarity in the Polynesian name of *Maru* can only be accidental. And I may add that in Estonian also we find storm-gods *Marutu uled* or *maro*, plural *marud*." This in sum represents the approach by the Indologists from the West supported by Indian scholarship of Sayana's persuasion.[1] But is that

[1] There are, indeed, other viewpoints, for instance, the Biological theory. To the exponents of this view, "(The Maruts) arise from the Pons which is personified as Rudra...sons of Prishni, the cow, which is probably the region underneath the corpus callosum, which has the appearance of a cow...regions of birth of the Maruts are anatomically comparable to the mid-brain and the Pons in which twelve pairs of cerebral nerves have their origin. These cerebral

all? If the Maruts are simply the Storm-powers in Nature, the strong winds whose depradations are so well-known to everyone, what are we to make of utterances of the Rishis, when they say, for instance:

---

nerves carry impressions from the organs of sense as well as their secretions. They are a group of motor, sensory motor and secretory nerves. From these, their various abodes, the Maruts spread through the airy region towards the two heavens, the cerebral hemispheres, which appear to be standing by them as the goddess Rodasi, to be wooed by them in order that they may gain consciousness of their own activities...These nerves are like brothers who come into activity simultaneously and are therefore equal in age. They are of one mind as the task of every nerve is to carry afferent impressions to the cerebral cortex, Indra...these cerebral nerves of Maruts create storm-clouds in the form of desires which smite the earth, i.e., the spinal chord, like lightning and produce a craving for the satisfaction of desires. This craving causes the heavenly canopy of Brahma (the brain) to tremble at the raging of the clouds and shake the tree of the voluntary nerves to send efferent impules along them to the earthly regions for the satisfaction of desires." (*Vide* V. G. Rele: *The Vedic Gods as Figures of Biology*, Pp. 55-57.)

There is also an interesting reading of Sri T. Paramasiva Iyer in his book *Riks*. Parallels are drawn between the description of the Maruts, their lineage, their activities and forms given in the Hymns and the natural phenomena on the snowy tops of mountains. The Maruts are these snows, snow-fields and snow-storms. "Rudra is the electricity with which the atmosphere in the high mountain is charged and is associated with the production of snows.. (Prishni) is the cirrus cloud... never descends to the earth but ever floats above the highest mountains...Rudra and the Maruts are great healers and medicine men as a snow-storm accompanied by copious discharge of electricity clears and purifies earth and air and makes medicinal herbs spring up like magic...the snow avalanche is the sudden movement of the Maruts without car or horses." (Pp. 17-19)

But we need not enter into a consideration of these or similar theories that are advanced in the field. That would be beside our purpose which is to see if the Maruts have a spiritual and psychological character in the hymns of the Veda.

He is a sage, the illumined thinker, Dhira, who knows these mysteries the mighty Prishni bore in her udder.[1]

Seeing the forms, activities, vehicles, etc., of the Maruts, Vasishtha is overcome with wonder at their mysterious character,—*niṇyāni*, he says, a word which in the Rig Veda constantly signifies what is secret, concealed, mystery,—and exclaims that only a sage, a person who has received the higher illumination in his mind and sight, can know of them. Now there is nothing at all concealed or secret about the doings of the storm-winds. These natural phenomena could hardly be the *ninyāni* which are known only to the enlightened sage.

Or again, when Seer Agastya sings,

With strongholds hundredfold, O Maruts, shield ye well from ruin and from sin, the man whom you have loved,[2]

how are we to understand the Maruts' protection from sin, *aghāt rakṣata*? "If the Rishi appeases the Maruts—the material phenomena, the storms—by his praise, his dwelling-places and other possessions may be rendered safe from the attack of furious storms (and he may be said to be saved from ruin). But if they be simply the natural phenomena how is it possible for them to be instinct with conscious activity and inner functioning that eliminates sin?" (Sri Kapali Sastriar)[3].

---

[1] *etāni dhīro niṇyā ciketa pṛṣniryadūdho mahī jabhāra* |
Rv. VII. 56. 4. (Tr. by Sri Kapali Sastriar)

[2] *śatabhujibhistamabhihrutiraghāt pūrbhi rakṣatā maruto yamāvata* || (Rv. I. 166. 8)

Unless otherwise mentioned, all the English renderings of Riks in this study are adapted from the available translations by Griffth, Wilson, Max Muller, etc.

[3] Rig Veda Bhashya.

Who, then, are the Maruts? The Rishis themselves ask this question again and again. Let us see how they answer it.

II

Before proceeding further on the subject let us make it clear that the system of symbolic interpretation we follow in our study of the Vedic Hymns is aimed at getting to the esoteric or inner significance of the Vedic Gods, their characteristic activities in the cosmos and in the individual. This does not necessarily negative the validity of other possible lines of interpretation, for example, the naturalistic. As in the case of other Gods, so with the Maruts also, the naturalistic interpretation can hold good; but only as far as their external character is concerned. There is something more, in fact much more behind it and that is, as we shall see, the real, the central truth of these deities who are so repeatedly invoked by the Vedic Rishi in the course of the pilgrimage of his soul from mortality to Immortality. These powers of movement, of irresistible strength that smashes all obstruction, Forces that set aflow currents of waters from the ocean below as well as from the ocean above, these deities in whose wake follows a trail of light, in whose life-filled bounty all thirst and hunger disappear—these are, to the ancient mystics, Divine Powers that have a definite part to play in the building up of their inner life. In the words of Sri Aurobindo, these "luminous and violent gods of the storm and lightning, uniting in themselves the power of Vayu, the Wind, the Breath, the Lord of Life and the force of Agni, the Seer-Will, are therefore seers who do the work by the knowledge, *kavayo vidmanā apasaḥ*, as well as battling forces who by the power of the heavenly Breath and the heavenly lightning overthrow the established things, the artificial obstructions, *kṛtrimāṇi rodhāmsi* in which the sons of darkness have entrenched themselves and aid Indra to overcome Vritra and the Dasyus. They seem to be in the esoteric Veda the Life-powers that support by their nervous or vital energies the action of the thought in the attempt of the mortal consciousness to grow or expand itself into the Immortality of the Truth and Bliss."

Let us now turn to the Riks of the Rishis themselves.

Who are these resplendent leaders, of common dwelling, young heroes of Rudra, borne by graceful steeds?[1]

Seeing the host of Maruts, struck with their brilliance, their youth and their horses, and the oneness of their station, Vasishtha asks, who they could be? They are, he says, radiant and self-luminous; their form bespeaks a manifesting light. And light, in the Veda, is the form and symbol of knowledge. That is, they are self-revealing in the fullness of the knowledge they embody. They are leaders: they do not wait upon events; they lead the way which they—sons of Rudra—open up in their vigour for the benefit of their suppliant. And powerful though they be, each of them, they are, says the seer, one-homed; they are all born and they live together in the same abode—the *antarikṣa*; living together, they act together. Their strengths work in harmony. They are borne on *horses*. *Aśva*, horse, in the Veda signifies power, life-force and indicate dynamic energy for action. These horses, the powers or energies on which they ride, are graceful; they are not wild and uncouth. They have a beauty of perfection. Who are

---

[1] *ka īm vyaktā naraḥ sanīḷā rudrasya maryā adhā svaśvāḥ* ||
(Rv. VII. 56. 1)

they, these leaders distinguished for their light of knowledge, power for action and oneness of origin and functioning?

Verily, no one knoweth of their birth; they, and they only, know each other's birth.[1]

It goes without saying, says the Rishi, that no one knows of their birth. Where they were born, when and to whom, are questions that man cannot answer. One has to address the Gods themselves, because they alone in their knowledge know their origin and the purpose for which they are manifest. Each of them knows not only of himself but of all the rest also because they are of one origin, one abode. Each of them is so much interconnected with the others that the knowledge of one forms also the knowledge of the other.

He describes them further. He is so much fascinated by their sight that as he wonders who they could be and whence their birth, he sees some more of the striking things about them.

They bestrew each other with light; rumbling like the wind these birds excel each other."[2]

They are luminous singly, but much more so in company. Each one shares his light of knowledge with the other: each nourishes his fellows with his own light, this resulting in a mutual enrichment and a common increase of Light. They shine and outshine each other in form and beauty. Their movement in battalions sounds *like* the

---

[1] *nakirhyeṣām janūṃṣi veda te anga vidre mitho janitram* ||
(Rv. VII. 56. 2)

[2] *abhi svapūbhirmitho vapanta vātasvanasaḥ śyenā aspṛdhan* ||
(Rv. VII, 56. 3)

rumble of the wind, *vāyuvat*. And swiftly coursing in the wide expanses, the planes of Life and the firmaments of Mind, they recall to the Rishi the image of birds winging through the sky. He is amazed at these wonders about the Maruts, their brilliances, their beautiful forms and comely horses, their movement and their sound; they, he asserts, are mysteries, *niṇyani*, secrets, and goes on to reflect:

He is a sage, the illumined thinker, Dhira, who knows these mysteries the mighty Prishni bore in her udder.

The Maruts are indeed born of the womb of the great Mother, the famous Prishni; yet, the common man, observes the seer, cannot know of them. To perceive the truths about them one needs to be a thinker; not merely one whose mental faculties are well developed, but one who has received the higher illumination that lights up the objects of knowledge, a sage whose wisdom is suffused with the Light from on High.

And here is Shyavashva Atreya asking the same question:

Who knows the birth of these or who was of yore in the grace of the Maruts when harnessed were the spotted deer?[1]

Does any one know who the Maruts are by birth, where they were born? Or is there any body who has known personally of their beneficence, who has 'sat in their high beatitudes'? The benevolence of the Maruts is opened on the worshipper when their cars of movement are yoked with the spotted deer, the fleeting antelopes of life-energies. One who has known of their benevolence

---

[1] *ko veda jānameṣām ko vā purā sumneṣvāsa marutām |*
yadyuyuja kilāsyaḥ || (Rv. V. 53. 1)

must have known of their powers, of their strengths as well.[1] Who can that blessed person be, wonders the seer.

Who has heard them, when they mounted the chariots, how they went forth? Who is the bounteous man for whom their kindred streams of waters flowed down with words of Revelation?[2]

If it requires an uncommon eye, an illumined sight to get a glimpse of the Hosts of Maruts, it is also only a specially gifted ear that can listen to their sound of movement and make out in what direction they speed on their chariots. Who is such a man as has heard them?

The advent of the Maruts is followed by their kinsmen, the waters that flow in profusion. The Waters symbolise the currents of the Conscious Being. They flow only to the bounteous man; that is, he who keeps nothing for himself like a miser, but gives and gives largely what he owns to the Gods, to the Universal Powers, the rightful owners of all that man possesses. The Maruts and the waters are kinsmen because both of them—the powers of life and thought, and the flowing currents—derive from the same sea of Consciousness that is at the base of all Existence. The subtle powers of Life, as they are set working in the Yajna, the inner sacrifice of the Yajamana, the worshipper, rise to the higher levels of Thought, impart their nerve-force to its movements and initiate an upward thrust which brings down the floods of the Higher Consciousness, the *waters* that are instinct with the light of the Divine Mind above and pour into the being of the

---

[1] *tadeṣām sthitim balalakṣaṇāni sukhāni ca ko jānāti* |
...(Sayana)

[2] *etān ratheṣu tasthuṣaḥ kaḥ śuśrāva kathā yayuḥ* |
kasmai sasruḥ sudāse anvāpaya ilabhirvṛṣṭayah saha ||
(Rv. V. 53. 2)

worshipper words of revelation, *iḷābhiḥ*.[1] The Revealed Word, the *śruti*, is thus vouchsafed, not to any one in the raw, but only to one who has by a progressive inner growth lifted up the dynamism of his life-being to the level of the mind, imparted its energy to the upward soaring thought-aspirations and thus equipped himself to receive the Word.

Whoever knows this, asks the Rishi. And then with a candour free from the inhibitions of sophistication, with an accent of happy affirmation—a feature that is so characteristic of the seers of the Veda—he proclaims:

To me they told it, and they came with winged steeds radiant, to the draught,

Youths, Heroes, free from spot or stain: Behold us here and praise thou us.[2]

What he aspired to know, the Rishi recalls, they the Maruts themselves made him know. They revealed the the truth of themselves to his being. They did so, he adds, when they came on their rapid and shining chargers to partake of the feast, the offering of his life's Soma, the essence of the delight of his existence churned out by him in *tapasyā* from his own life-experiences and realisations. The revelation of the truth of the godheads is complete only when the self-offering of the human individual is rendered hearty and delectable—without

---

[1] Ila is the goddess of truth-vision or Revelation. 'Ila the strong primal word of the Truth who gives us its active vision'. (Sri Aurobindo)

'Ila the Inspiration that expresses truth-vision in vocal terms.' (Sri Kapali Sastriar: *Further Lights: The Veda and the Tantra.*)

[2] *te mā āhurya āyayurupa dyubhirvibhirmade* |
naro maryā arepasa imanpaśyanniti ṣṭuhi || (Rv. V 53. 3)

any sense of loss or sacrifice—and shaped into the draught of Bliss that is ever enchanting to the Gods. And how were they? They were youthful; for all the ceaseless activity they have been engaged in as cosmic functionaries, as powers who have been long at work in releasing themselves from the hold of inertia and inconscience of Matter, they had not aged. They are always young and fresh because they are sustained by the gushing streams of the force of consciousness at their fount. They were heroic but for all their fury and violence they were not tainted with evil. Their heroism and strength are aimed only at what obstructs the path of the Truth, the spread of the Light. Their horses were rapid in speed and radiant in form: they were borne on the fullnesses of the force of life charged with the glistening light of illumination. *They told him*: Here we are, look into us, look for yourself who we are. And doubtless they endowed him with the vision with which alone he could know them. Not verbal knowledge but knowledge by direct perception was what the Maruts gave him. And they asked him to chant their glory. *Stuti*, prayer in eulogy, is dear to the Gods—it is called the food of the Gods—not because it is flattering to their own sense of importance on human analogy, but more truly because when sincere, it is an expression of a deeper realisation on the part of the aspiring soul of the greatness of the Adored, a vivid perception of the truths embodied in Him, and in the very act of expression an effective means for the worshipper to open a channel of communication with and grow into the very Person of the Invoked. The Deity who is thus addressed with fervour responds and in time *grows*, grows into the being of worshipper; *they (prayers) increase Indra*, says a Rik.[1] The Maruts asked the

[1] *indram nakṣantīdabhi vardhayantīḥ* | (Rv. VI. 34. 3)

Rishi to chant the hymn of praise so as to give a concrete shape to and thus firmly establish the fact of his realisation of their truth.

The same Seer declares elsewhere:

They, the impellers, when asked their kin, named the Cow, named the Prishni, as their mother; and the impetuous Rudra, they the Mighty Ones, declared their Father.[1]

The Maruts are the *impellers.*[2] "Of all that was of old and of all that is new, of all that rises from the soul and all that seeks expression, they are the impellers." "(They) are powers of will and nervous or vital Force that have attained to the light of thought and the voice of self-expression. They are behind all thought and speech as its impellers and they battle towards the Light, Truth and Bliss of the supreme Consciousness." (Sri Aurobindo) When the Rishi asked them of their lineage, they declared Prishni, the Cow, to be their mother. Who is Prishni? She is taken by modern scholars to be 'Many-coloured earth' following Sayana or as 'speckled cloud'. In the *Nighantu*, however, Prishni stands for the sky—and this takes us nearer the conception of the Vedic mystic to whom Prishni, the dappled Cow, symbolises Aditi of the mid-region, the sky. "Their (Maruts') mother is the Cow of variegated hue which means symbolically the Shakti who is the field for the manifestation of the Life-power, who contains in her womb the rays of thought-power, who fills the mid-region with her

---

[1] *pra ye me bandhveṣe gām vocanta sūrayaḥ pṛṣnim vocanta mātaram |*
aghā pitaramiṣmiṇam rudram vocanta śikvasaḥ |
(Rv. V. 52. 16)

[2] *sūrayaḥ prerakāḥ* (Sayana)

infinite extension as Aditi, endowed with capacities for bringing out diverse manifestations, the multi-hued Cow, Prishni, the mother of Maruts." (Sri Kapali Sastriar)[1]. The Maruts are also described as *gomātaraḥ*, children of the Cow,[2] the Cow of course standing for the Infinite Consciousness whose form is Light; they are also called *sindhumātaraḥ*,[3] children of the Rivers, the streams of Consciousness. The point is the Maruts are born of the Higher Consciousness in manifestation. The place of their birth is the mid-region, *antarikṣa*, the plane of Life. But to that we shall come later. They declared Rudra the impetuous to be their father. Rudra is the God of Wrath, of irresistible fury which brooks no obstacle. " (*Rudra*) the Mighty one of Heaven...is the violent one who leads the upward evolution of the conscious being; his force battles against all evil, smites the sinner and the enemy; intolerant of defect and stumbling he is the most terrible of the gods, the one of whom alone the Vedic Rishis have any real fear...The Maruts, vital powers which make light for themselves by violence are Rudra's children. Agni and Maruts are the leaders of the fierce struggle upward from Rudra's first earthly, obscure creation to the heavens of thought, the luminous worlds." (Sri Aurobindo). If as children of Prishni the Maruts are shapings of the streams of Consciousness, as the offspring of Rudra, they are the manifestations of Force.

Or, to take a Rik from Bharadwaja:

They who are Sons of Bounteous Rudra, whom the long lasting One had strength to foster;

---

[1] Rig Veda Bhashya.

[2] Rv. I. 85. 3

[3] Rv. X. 78. 6

They Mighty Ones whose germ great Mother Prishni is known to have received for man's advantage.[1]

Here again, the Maruts are the progeny of Rudra and Prishni. But Rudra is described as the bounteous. Rudra is not the terrible only. "This violent and mighty Rudra who breaks down all defective formations and groupings of outward and inward life, has also a benigner aspect. He is the supreme healer. Opposed, he destroys; called on for aid and propitiated he heals all wounds and all evil and all sufferings. The force that battles is his gift, but also the final peace and joy." (Sri Aurobindo). The Maruts inherit this benignity of Rudra —even as they are imbued with his violence—and hence they are known as healers.[2] To bear his seed it required a womb of unparalleled strength and vitality. And whose else could that be but that of the mighty Mother extended in the mid-region whence flow all currents of power and life, the Creatrix of variegated hue? And she received it, says the Rishi, for the benefit of man. In the upward movement of the human soul there are certain obstructions and impediments to be overcome, certain upliftings and sublimations of the lower energies and movements to be effected, and some positive states established which are all well beyond human capacity to achieve unaided. To fulfil these imperative demands of the striving spirit and lead man further up the ladder of his progress, the Maruts are brought into manifestation. They are the gods that preside over the subtle life-

---

[1] *rudrasya ye mīhḷuṣah santi putrā yānśco nu dādhṛvirbharadhyai |*
vide tė mātā maho māhī ṣā setpṛśniḥ subhvė garbhamādhāt ||
(Rv. VI. 66. 3)

[2] *mārutasya bheṣajasya āvahata* | (Rv. VIII. 20. 23)

energies and thought-powers. It is for this indispensable purpose of man that Prishni bore them in her womb and fostered after birth. That, adds the Rishi, is well known. This manifestation, their birth in man, the seeker engaged in the inner Yajna, is an event of capital importance. Listen to Seer Kanva:

O ye Maruts, ye the sons whom Prishni bore, when ye are born (in) mortals, then immortal would be your worshipper.[1]

Ordinarily the life-energies in man are turned towards the satisfaction of the demands of the body dominated by the desire-self. Even when the purposes to which they are directed are less physical and pertain to the domain of the vital and the mental *puruṣas*, they are nonetheless used in the service of the surface-being. But once one turns to the higher life, aspires and endeavours to turn all of oneself towards that Ideal, the life-energies naturally begin to re-orient themselves. As they draw back from the surface, from the gross physical pre-occupations, they begin to assume more and more of their natural character; they are subtilised, they move more freely on the subtler levels of the being. They turn upward and inward and share in the general aspiration and the response it evokes from the higher and inner Powers. They uplift themselves and acquire the freedom and right to move up to the level of the mind, they attain the light of the thought, and in their increase on that plane impart their own power, their impulsions and nervous strengths to the thought movements which are already aspiring to reach out—but fail for want of sufficient driving force—to the still higher regions of the illumined mentality, the domain

[1] *yadyūyam pṛṣnimātaro matasiḥ syātana |*
stotā vo amṛtaḥ syāt || (Rv. I. 38. 4)

of the Divine Mind, Indra. The impetus given by the life-powers now identified with and sustaining them gives them the necessary dynamism to force their way against all obstruction and grow into illumined thought-powers. This in brief is the birth of the Maruts in man, their second birth as it is called, the first being their original manifestation in the Cosmos. We will have occasion to refer to this again while dealing with the relation of the Maruts with Gods like Indra. With this birth of the Maruts in the worshipper, says the seer, the eventual success in attaining the goal of Immortality is assured. The whole multitude of the Thought-forces energised by the uplifted powers of life have entered into the Light of the Divine-Mind, taken birth on the mental summits of the worshipper, a victory of crucial importance registered. With the liberation of these two important parts of his, viz. his life-being and the mind-being, from subjection to inertia, limitation, incapacity, ignorance and falsehood, the worshipper is on the assured step towards the Vedic immortality which is "a vast beatitude, a large enjoyment of the divine and infinite existence reposing on a perfect union between the Soul and Nature; the Soul becomes King of itself and its environment, conscious on all its planes, master of them, with Nature for its bride delivered from divisions and discords into an infinite and luminous harmony." (Sri Aurobindo)[1].

They sprang to birth from the sky, lofty Ones, pourers, sons of Rudra, conquerors of their foes;

---

[1] This Rik has been translated by western scholars in a variety of ways but by none in the directness of the original. And the reasons for it are interesting. *Vide* note by Max Muller: "One might translate: 'If you, sons of Prishni, were mortals, then immortal would be your worshipper.' But this seems almost too deep and elaborate a compliment for a primitive age"!

Purifiers, shining bright as the (rays of) the sun, powerful as giants, dripping, awful of form.[1]

They are born of the sky, the mid-region between the Earth and the Heaven, where, as we have noted earlier, the Infinite Consciousness Aditi is extended as Prishni of many-hued form. It is because of this their birth from the mid-air that they are classified among the gods of the mid-region, *madhyamasthānāḥ*[2], they who *know* the mighty region of mid-air—the Plane of Life. The Maruts are thus primarily powers of the Life-plane, they derive their strength and impetuosity from the Life-Force that governs the region. The might with which these sons of Rudra extirpate their adversaries, the strength and fury with which these stalwarts of terrible visage match the boundless power of the legions of non-terrestrial beings that abound in the occult worlds, are derived from this reservoir of dynamism in the creation. And yet, they are sinless, without blemish (an epithet which can hardly be applied to the all-wrecking storms of thunder and lightning in Nature); their violence, the 'lofty aggressions' are carried out in the force of the bright Light to which they have attained. Like the rays of the Sun (of spiritual Truth), the radiations of the light in which they are clothed illumine and vivify those whom they touch. In the force of their movement they rake up and throw out the dross of ignorance and inertia from their field

---

[1] *te jajhire diva ṛśvāsa ukṣaṇo rudrasya maryā asura arepasaḥ | pāvakāsaḥ śucayaḥ sūryā iva sattvāno na drapsino ghoravarpasaḥ ||* (Rv. I 64.2)

[2] *athātho madyamasthānā devagaṇāh |*
teṣām marutaḥ prathamagāmino bhavanti || (Nirukta II 2.1)
maruto ha vai devaviśo'antarikṣabhāianā īśvarāḥ| (Kau. Br. 7.8)
ye maho rajaso viduḥ | (Rv. I. 19.3)

and render it pure. They drip with the waters of purified life-energies and illumined thought-energies and pour them in torrents on the soil of the human soul.

Their number is significant.

The mighty Ones, the seven times seven, have each given me a hundred.

In the Yamuna I bathe the ȷamed wealth in kine and wealth in steeds.[1]

The troops of the Maruts are frequently spoken as seven in number.[2] Seven, we must note, is a mystic number in the Indian and other ancient traditions. In the Veda, we find it applied to many objects, e.g., *sapta gāvaḥ* seven cows; *sapta sindhavah*, seven rivers; *saptà sānavaḥ*, seven hills; *saptaḥ arciṣaḥ*, seven flames; *sapta rasmayaḥ*, seven rays etc. The Rishis perceived seven fundamental principles of existence in the Creation. In their conception the creative Reality formulated itself in seven tiers, from the highest to the lowest rung,—and each level or plane of creation was governed by its own principle of being. Thus they speak of the sevenfold creation consisting of the three divine worlds above, the three cosmic divisions below, with the Greater Heaven, *bṛhat dayauḥ*, in between. These seven worlds are characterised by their seven ruling psychological principles or

---

[1] *sapta me saptaśākina ekamekā śatā daduḥ* |
yamunāyāmadhi śrutamudradho gavyam mṛjē ni radho aśvyam mṛje || (Rv. V. 52. 17)

[2] *sapta hi maruto gaṇāḥ* (*sa. bra.* 5. 4. 3. 17)
saptagaṇā vai marutah (*va. ya.* 1. 6. 2. 3; 2. 7. 2. 2)
sapta sapta hi mārutā gaṇā | (*va. ya.* 17. 80-85);
sa. bra. 9. 3. 1. 25)

forms of existence, *Sat*, Being; *Cit*, Consciousness; *Ananda*, Delight; *Vijñāna*, Truth-Knowledge; *Manas*, Mind; *Prana*, Life; and *Annam*, Matter. All was conceived in terms of these seven strands of Being. And, naturally, the Maruts, the armies of aspiring forces are referred to in sevens (and multiples of seven), each appropriate to its own level. As Sri Aurobindo observes in another connection: "Seven is the number of essential principles in manifested Nature, the seven forms of divine consciousness at play in the world. Each formulated severally, contains the other six in itself; thus the full number is 49."

They are the mighty Ones who can do anything, *sarvamapi kartum śaktāḥ* (Sayana), achieve even what is impossible to human capacity. They gave him,—*each of them*, says the Rishi, to emphasise the distinctive character of the gifts given severally, seven times—a Hundred. Hundred signifies a completeness, a fullness, wholeness without a breach. The gifts were thus complete leaving no want unfulfilled. What were the gifts? It is the famed riches, the celebrated plenitude in the giving of the Gods, the wealth of Cows, the wealth of Horses. We have seen in our studies before that in the Veda, Cow is the outer image of Light, not physical light but the Light of Knowledge. Similarly Horse symbolises power, force, dynamis of activity. Both these image Consciousness in the form of Knowledge and Consciousness in the form of Force. Thus the complete gifts bequeathed to the Rishi by the hosts of the Maruts are the treasures of Knowledge and Power. And what he proceeds to do with them is revealing. He bathes them in the Yamuna. Yamuna, the hallowed river of sacred waters would seem to signify the streams of the deepest consciousness of being; to the salve of these pristine waters the Rishi submits all the god-given wealth of Knowledge and Power. He keeps nothing apart, he dedicates all to the Supreme Purpose.[1]

Thus far regarding the origin and birth of the Maruts. We shall next deal with their brilliant form and Coat of mail, their weapons and their vehicles, their feats in war and their missions of mercy.

---

[1] *Vide* Sri Aurobindo: A Hymn of the Thought Gods (*On the Veda*) "Seven and seven the Thought-gods came to me and seven times they gave me a hundredfold; in Yamuna I will bathe the shining herds of my thoughts which they have given, I will purify my swiftnesses in the river of my soul."

THE MARUTS (II)

We have seen that in their psychological aspect, the Maruts are the aspiring forces in man, powers that are born of life and attain to the light of the purer mind. Combining in themselves the swiftnesses characteristic of Vayu, the God of the Life-plane, and the strength and force of Rudra who is their sire, it is the Maruts who give the necessary nerve-strengths, speed and drive to the inner being of the Vedic mystic in the ascent of his Yajna, Sacrifice, to the Goal of Immortality. As children of Aditi, the Infinite Consciousness extended in the etheric spaces, they are primarily the gods of the mid-region, *antarikṣa*, the world of life, but they arrive at their full stature only when they reach the heights of the mind proper and impart their energisms to the thought-movements seeking greater heights. They are always on the move in companies and are referred in sevens or multiples of seven, corresponding to the seven Planes in the hierarchy of Creation based on the seven Principles of Existence.

The Maruts are worthy of their birth.

Stable, indeed, is their birth-place; the birds are able to issue from their mother; for their strength everywhere is twofold.[1]

The strength of the Maruts, says the seer, is not confined to one region. It is spread everywhere. It is twofold, the power of knowledge and the power of action.[2] The Maruts possess these two elements of

---

[1] *sthiram hi jānameṣām vayo māturniretave |*
yat sīmanu dvitā śavaḥ || (Rv. I. 37.9)

[2] *prajnābalam bāhubalam ca* (Raghavendraswami: (*Mantrārthamanjari*)

knowledge and activity because of the very nature of their origin of birth. Though their mother, Prishni, is the source and field for the variegated play of the Life-force, she contains also in her womb the multitude of thought-powers; such is the greatness of their origin; it is *dhruva*, solid and firm, excellent.[1] The birds are the thought-powers. In the Veda we find many instances where these powers of thought are described as birds;[2] and birds here symbolise "energies...liberated and upsoaring, winging upward towards the heights of our being, winging widely with a free light, no longer involved in the ordinary limited movement." (Sri Aurobindo). They are so much instinct with the strength of their supporting life-energy that they are able to soar straight the moment they are born. Thus do the Maruts carry with them the double characteristic of their fount—Consciousness as force and Consciousness as knowledge.

The same truth is emphasised by another Rishi.

Here, here, ye of self-grown strength, seers with skin of Sun's splendour, O Maruts, I dedicate to you this sacrifice.[3]

The strength of the Maruts is their own, they do not derive their sustenance from outside. Their very substance is of strength, the force of life which in its native character knows no diminution. Its nature is to expand, to grow. And they are not merely of this self-growing strength. They are *kavayah*, seers, *krānta darśinah*, says Sayana; they who see what is *beyond*; they are

[1] *sthiratvena uttamatām lakṣāyati.* (*Mantrārthamanjari*)

[2] e.g. Rv. I 88.1; I. 87. 2; VII. 56.3.

[3] *iheha vaḥ svatavasa kanaya sūryatvaca |*
yajnam maruta ā vṛṇe ||
(Rv. VII. 59.11) Tr. by Sri Kapali Sastriar.

endowed with the knowledge-vision that transcends the senses; not only that, their very skin is of the light, the splendour of the Sun who stands, in the Veda, for the Supreme Truth and Knowledge. The Rays of this Sun of Truth, the spreadings of the Knowledge constitute the stuff of their natural covering. To such, says the Rishi, to such embodiments of Force and Knowledge, he dedicates the sacrifice of his life-endeavour, *here*, *here*, here now on earth.

"The Rishi says: 'Oh you Maruts, you gods are *svatavasaḥ*, grown of your own strength, *kavayah*, seers, *sūrya-tvacah*, the spelendour of the Sun itself is your covering and protective skin; to you, such as these, I dedicate today the sacrifice.' Now how could these seers—those who look beyond the past and the present and as such endowed with consciousness—be mere natural phenomenon of storms, entities without consciousness?" (Sri Kapali Sastriar)[1]

There is a constant emphasis on their quality of strength. Deriving as they do from the plane of Life which is the reservoir of all dynamic energies, the Maruts are filled with strength as a matter of course.

O ye of unfailing strength, make That manifest; strike the fiend with your lustrous might.[2]

The Maruts, the seer declares, have a strength which never fails to effectuate itself: it is true strength. It is lustrous like everything else that concerns the Maruts. He appeals to them to strike down the enemy, the evil ones who oppose, and thus clear the *way*. Way for what?

---

[1] Rig Veda Bhashya

[2] *yūyam tat satyaśavasa āviṣkarta mahitrana* |
vidhyatā vidyutā rakṣaḥ || (Rv. I. 86·9)

To manifest *That,* to bring into play the Great Light of which the subsequent Rik speaks, the Light which is the source of all Knowledge and Truth-Power.

Or again,

Bounteous givers, whole strength have ye; shakers (of earth), perject in your blazing might.

Maruts, against the wrathful enemv of the seers, let loose an enemy like a dart.[1]

Their strength is whole; it is not lacking in completeness. Limitation of any kind does not mar it. It is because of this fullness of strength that they are able to give fully, bounteously. The throb of their force shakes everything around: the earth, i.e. the body of the worshipper, trembles at the impact of their vibrant power. Their might which is brilliant with the glow of the informing Light is perfect in its sweep. To such exemplars of Strength and Might, the Rishi prays for action against the enemies of the seers, the forces of darkness and ignorance who are up in arms in anger against the worshipper,—mark the significant word *ṛṣi*, one who sights the liberating word—who is finding the means to free himself from their hold. He prays to the Maruts to let loose against them something of their enormous strength which is sure to strike and be effective as a pointed missile against an adversary.

If the Maruts are known for their unparalleled strength, they are no less distinguished for their wisdom.

---

[1] *asamyojo vibhṛtha sudānavósāmi dhūtayaḥ śāvaḥ |*
ṛṣidviṣe marutaḥ parimanyava iṣum na sṛ ͥata dviṣam ||
(Rv. I. 39.10)

The hymns in the Rig Veda repeat again and again that these gods are *kavayaḥ*, seers, their activities are governed by a lofty knowledge which is specially theirs. Here, for instance, is a Rik of Nodhas:

Grant us, O ye Maruts, wealth, durable, rich in prowess and speeding the fleeing foe. A hundred, yea, thousandfold, ever increasing!

May the host of the Maruts, Thought-wealthy, come soon and anon.[1]

The Maruts are *dhiyāvasu*, an epithet the Rishi uses in more than one Rik. Their wealth lies in their Thought. No doubt they are born of the substance of life and are primarily life-powers. Still, as Sri Aurobindo says, they are effective on the mental, the thought-plane. They begin their characteristic action when they grow and move on the heights of the mind, acquire the birthright of the Thought-land, themselves filling the region with their innate dynamis. This Thought, the characteristic movement or expression of the Consciousness that is at work as Intelligence on this level in Creation is brought into manifestation and fuller play by the Maruts; it is their wealth that the seer describes in significant adjectives which cannot apply to ordinary material wealth. It is durable; it is not fleeting and exhaustible. The substance of Thought rooted at its secret base in a principle of Infinite Knowledge exceeds the limitations of finite Space and Time. It has a dynamic power, charged with the impetuosity of the life-energies that have risen and joined

---

[1] *nū ṣṭhiram maruto vīravantamṛtīṣāmha rayimasmāsu dhatta* | *sahasriṇam śatinam śūśuvāmsam prātarmakṣū dhiyāvasurjagamyāt* || (Rv. I. 64.15)

to it. This element of force, apart from the Power which is inalienable from all true Thought, enable it to drive away the enemy, the darkness and ignorance vanishing with the dawn of Knowledge. It is hundred, thousand-fold i.e., it is varied, complete, not wanting in wholeness.[1] Even full, it does not stop content with its fullness; that is the feature of things in the lower creation of tamas and inertia. From fullness it pours into a greater fullness; the heights of the mental summits have no end; they go on expanding and ever expanding.[2] Such is the wealth for which the Maruts are known and the seer beseeches them for an early call at the altar of his soul.

Or to take another Rik:

They carry with them the sweetness (of Ananda) as their eternal offspring, and play out their play brilliant in the activities of knowledge.[3]

With the harmony attained between the swell of life-energy and the poise of the purified mental Thought open to Knowledge,—for that is what the awakening and play of the Maruts in the seeker means—there is a natural outflow of happiness, a streaming of sweet joy which always accompanies the manifestation of the Maruts; they are *mayobhuvaḥ* giving birth of Delight. But they do not rest tranquil in the enjoyment of this ananda. They are essentially powers of movement, *yayiyaḥ*,[4] powers

---

[1] *rāyaḥ......na yo yucchati...... sahasriṇam* wealth in thousands which never vanishes (Rv. V. 54.13)

[2] *asya dhiyaḥ prāvitā* (The host of Maruts) increaser of our intellect (Rv. I. 87.4)

[3] *nityam na sūnum madhu bibhrata upakrīḷanti krīlā vidathuṣu ghṛṣvayaḥ* | (Rv. I. 166.2) Tr. by Sri Aurobindo

[4] Rv. X. 78.7

that seek and embody, seek yet more and manifest. Theirs is the play of the winning and the giving of the treasures of Knowledge, of Light, which are massed on the heights of the Divine Mind.[1] They win the illuminations of higher Knowledge and make them effective and active in the person of the sacrificer.[2] In the words of Sri Aurobindo: The Maruts "are energies which make for knowledge. Theirs is not the settled truth, the diffused light, but the movement, the search, the lightning flash, and, when Truth is found, the many-sided play of its separate illuminations."

The might of the Maruts is irresistible because it is of another nature than that of the human kind.

Passing glorious must be your warrior might, not the guileful strength of the mortal.[3]

The prowess of man, however great it could be, is after all rooted in ignorance, in limited and even malformed knowledge that is falsehood; as long as he lives under their rule his actions continue to be coloured with that infirmity of nature. The might of the Maruts, the seer says, is not of that nature; it is free from the falsity of appearances, it has the nobility of warrior-make, it has a directness derived from its source in Truth,[4] and is hence supremely adorable, *atiśayena stotavyam* (Sayana), unlike the tainted human kind. These purified life-powers and thought-powers are not subject to the limit-

---

[1] *dadāśuṣe divaḥ koṣamacucyavuḥ*, they have cast the Heaven's treasury down for the worshipper's behoof. (Rv. V. 53. 6)

[2] *vidatheṣu dhīrāḥ*, wise thinkers in the discoveries of knowledge (Rv. III. 26.6)

[3] *yuṣmākamastu taviṣī panīyasī mā martyasya māyinaḥ* ||
(Rv. I. 39.2)

[4] *ṛtajatā arepasaḥ* (Rv. V. 61.14)

ing and twisting holds of Maya that so much characterise the formations on the physical plane. Theirs is the course of a large freedom moving towards the Law of the Truth.

Maruts, bright yourselves, bright are the offerings; to you the bright, I offer the bright sacrifice.

By Law they came to Truth, the observers of Law, of happy birth, bright, purifiers.[1]

The Maruts are bright, gleaming in their purity of form, and the offerings of the worshipper to be acceptable to them have to be of appropriate purity; they must be full of the light of the higher consciousness attained by the offerer, bright. The bright gods presiding over the purified and purifying energies on the life and the mental levels of the seeker will accept only the sacrifice that is aglow with the fire of aspiration. They arrive at the Truth, the Truth that is at the head of things, the Truth of themselves and the Truth of what is beyond them, by the *ṛtam*, the Law, the Right, the Way of the Truth-working. They are the observers of the Law, they move effortlessly on the Path of the Right and fail not to arrive at the Goal of the Truth. One who delivers himself into their hands is speeded up on this Path; happy is the moment when they are born in man,[2] for then it is possible for him to entrust his sacrifice to the charge of these toiling divinities who purify under the stress of their surging movement and brighten with their

---

[1] *śucī vo havyā marutaḥ sucīnām śucim hinomyadhvaram śucibhyaḥ* |
ṛtena satyamṛtasāpa āyanchucijanmānaḥ śucayaḥ pāvakāḥ ||
(Rv. VII. 56.12.)

[2] *bhadrajānayaḥ*, whose births make for happy good (Rv. V. 6.14)

own lustre of knowledge and power the inner being of the Yajamana set for the upward climb.

The same characteristics of the Maruts find expression in the utterance of another Rishi:

Ho, Maruts, Heroes, be gracious unto us, rich in treasures, immortal, knowers of the Law, Ye hearers of the Truth, seers, youthful, of mighty speech, grown mighty.[1]

The Maruts are spoken of in their many-sided opulence. They abound in treasures, their own wealth of kine and horses, of knowledge and power; they hold in themselves the truth of immortality into which it is open to their worshipper to grow. They are *knowers*, they know the Divine Law which governs All. They are *satyaśrutaḥ*, they who *hear* the Truth, who are open to the divine audition, the inspirations of Truth. They are also *seers*, the Wise that see with the eye of knowledge[2] through the barriers of Time and Space; they are full of youth, getting their sustenance from the ever-fresh fount of the waters of life-energies. Their speech, their voice, is powerful, it cannot be kept back,[3] their echoing utterances are mighty of result.[4] Full of their varied plenitude they grow ever and ever mightier for the benefit of the supplicant who waits upon their pleasure.

---

[1] *haye naro maruto mṛ.atā nastuvīmaghāsī amṛto ṛtajnāḥ |*
satyaśrutaḥ kavayo yuvāno bṛhadgirayo bṛhadukṣamāṇāḥ ||
(Rv. V. 58.8).

[2] *sūracakṣasaḥ* (Yajurveda 25.20)

[3] *na yo varāya marutāmivā svanaḥ* (Rv. I. 143.5)

[4] *bṛhad-girayaḥ* has been also translated as dwelling on lofty mountains. These Powers attain to their full states and acquire individuation on the higher altitudes—the summits of the Mind—of the Hill of being; they are their natural habitat.

The weapons of the Maruts, the means wherewith they destroy and build are as varied as they are spectacular. Their speech itself is a force of consequence.

Sing glory to the host of Maruts, brilliant, leaning to our praises, they of the flaming Word;

May they be exalted here in us.[1]

Theirs is the *Word* that signifies a concentrated expression of spiritual force in a sound-body. The voice of the Maruts is loaded with the power of the flaming Word, they are the singers of the Word, *brahmāṇo marutaḥ*, which breaks into the strongholds of the elements that oppose the onward progress of man and shatters their ramparts of blindness and obscurity. These Gods of the purified life and mind energies not only break down the evil by the force of their speech, but also affirm and help to establish the Truth in the being of the seeker by its power; the being of the Yajamana has to learn to put itself in tune with the music of these leaders of the journey if it would be wafted along on their brilliant course. "The shining host has arisen in my soul, the host of the Thought-gods and they sing a hymn as they march upward, a hymn of the heart's illumination. March thou on, O my soul, impetuously to their violent and mighty music. For they are drunk with the joy of an inspiration ...their thunders are the chant of the hymn of the gods and the proclamations of the Truth." (Sri Aurobindo).

The Maruts of the illumined Word, says the seer, are avid of worship. They look for the heart's adoration and its expression in speech from the worshipper because that is the one sure means whereby they can enter in

---

[1] *vandasva mārutam gaṇam tveṣam panasyumarkinam* |
asme vṛddhā asanniha || (Rv. I. 38.15)

communication and grow in his person with all the untold beneficence that goes with them. By that they will be exalted, their sway will increase in us, the Rishi says, here itself, *iha*, in the sacrifice which is in progress.

By the *word*, by their chants of power, the Maruts invoke the still higher godheads and their gifts upon the Sacrifice, upon the worshipper in whom they have been awakened into activity.

Who are brave, unsurpassed in strength, who laud in worship, O Agni, with them, the Maruts come.[1]

The Rishi calls upon Agni, the Seer-Will, to come to the sacrifice along with the Maruts who chant the Rik, celebrate the worship. Sayana would have it that *arka* is water;[2] Skandaswamin that it is Indra. In either case, as Sri Kapali Sastriar points out, the fact remains that the *word* of the Maruts is a fulfilling agent in the inner sacrifice of the Yajamana.[3] "Brothers of Indra, the brave Maruts are able to raise the word (of the Yajamana) to a high intensity of power, to reach to Indra the showerer of all wealth, or, to impel the currents of the Divine Powers symbolised by the *Waters*."[4]

---

[1] *ya ugrā arkamānṛcuranādhṛṣṭāsa ojasā* |
marudbhiragna ā gahi || (Rv. I. 19.4)

[2] *Vide* Max Muller's Note: "Sayana explains *arka* by water...... But *arka* has only received this meaning of water in the artificial system of interpretation first started by the authors of the Brahmanas, who had lost all knowledge of the natural sense of the ancient hymns."

[3] *Vide* also Rv. I. 52.15 where the Maruts are referred to as stirring Indra with their lauds when he is engaged in battle with the Enemy, Vritra the leading Force that obstructs.

[4] Rig Veda Bhashya

Creators of speech, they spread out wide the Waters in their courses; they urge the lowing kine to enter (the Waters) up to their knees.[1]

The Maruts have set out on their courses. They are the impellers, the creators of speech with which they fill the regions of their movement. Their speech, says the seer, is the precursor, the actuating cause of a development which has a special significance to the seeker. These companions of Indra, the Lord of the worlds who has the bounty of rain in his giving, initiate the downpour and spread out the Waters. The Waters signify the currents of Consciousness-Force which irrigate and fertilise the fields of the being of the worshipper. His path is flooded with these streams of Waters and the lowing *cows*, the infant rays of light which are beginning to show themselves on the horizons of the highest attained levels of the seeker, are urged by the Maruts with their impelling Words, to enter,—go in knee-deep and not stand out on the edge—into the Waters and drink and grow on their substance.[2]

There are numerous passages in the Rig Veda extolling the part of the Maruts in bringing down to the

---

[1] *udu tyē sūnavo giraḥ kāṣṭha ajmeṣvatnata |*
vāśrā abhijun yātave || (Rv. I. 37.10)

[2] Western scholars have needlessly confounded themselves on this Rik. The construction and meaning given by Sayana is unusually straight. *Sūnavaḥ* is to be taken, naturally, in the sense of impellers (*su preraṇe*); *vāca utpādakāḥ marutaḥ*, as the scholiast says. Again, *kāṣṭha* is here water, not wooden poles or enclosures as taken by some. Sayana quotes Yaska in justification: *āpopi kāṣṭha ucyante krāntvā sthithā bhavatīti* (Nirukta 2.15).

Earth the Waters[1] from Indra's world of Svar. They join Indra in their troops, increase his striking force with their powerful voice and irresistible strength and aid him to fell down the Coverer, Vritra, and release the imprisoned Waters of Consciousness and Force to stream forth and rain on the arid soil of the worshipper's being.[2] The Mystic looks to the Maruts to cause these Waters flow over not only those tracts of his existence which have been subjected to a continuous pressure of arduous discipline, *tapasya*, and prepared to fruitfully receive the showers from above, but also the other parts that have remained unresponsive, too dry and lifeless to participate in the general progress.[3] The streams which they pour down run in all directions, *viyadvartante enyaḥ*[4], and the entire being of the Yajamana is bathed in these Waters of rejuvenation and illumination.

The *speech* of the Maruts, however, is not of the ordinary kind. It requires a special faculty to be able to listen to the movements of self-expression of these Powers. Not every one can do it.

---

[1] *yūyam vṛṣṭim varṣayathā purīṣiṇaḥ*, Ye of Waters, pour the torrents down. (Rv. V. 55·5)

Vide also *sargā varṣasya varṣato varṣantu pṛthivīmanu*, May the Waters shed by the Maruts flow to the Earth. (Atharva 4·15). The Maruts themselves are *drapsāḥ purudrapsāḥ* dripping, dripping profusely.

[2] *anudhanvanāyanti vṛṣṭayaḥ* showers follow over desert spots (Rv. V. 53.6)

[3] Vide *śardho....mārutam tuviṣvaṇirapnasvatīṣūrvarāsviṣṭanirārtanāsviṣṭaniḥ*, an army of Life-Powers moving with fertilising rain over tilled and our waste lands. (Rv. I. 127.6) Tr. by Sri Aurobindo.

[4] Rv. V. 353.7

Wherever the Maruts pass, they fill the way with clamour. A rare one hears them.[1]

When the developing forces of the life and the thought-energies are on the move, their capacities for self-expression in terms and forms approprite to their kind are put into play in the stress of their growing might and freedom; and only some, the rare, observes the seer, can hear their report and benefit by it. The faculty of inner audition should have been opened up and trained in the course of the self-discipline for one to be able to recognise and receive their speech.

It is pertinent to ask whether this Rik would make sense if the sole truth of the Maruts is what is given the naturalistic interpretation. If the Maruts were nothing more than the storms and thunder in physical Nature, then why is it that *only some* can hear their words? Surely every one can hear the sound and fury of the elemental winds!

The Maruts are luminous not only in their own form, but in their weapons as well.

Thou, O Agni, was the first Angiras, the seer and auspicious friend, a god, of the gods, on the law of thy working the Maruts with their shining spears were born, seers who do the work by the knowledge.[2]

The Angirasas are the divine Flame powers who have the specific function of aiding Indra, the Lord of the

---

[1] *yaddha yanti marutaḥ sam ha bruvate' dhvanna* |
śṛnoti kaccideṣām || (Rv. I. 37.13)

[2] *tvamagne prathamo angirā ṛṣirdevo devānāmabhavaḥ śivaḥ sakhā* |
tava vrate kavayo vidmanapaso jāyanta maruto bhrājadṛṣṭayaḥ ||
(Rv. I. 31.1) Tr. by Sri Aurobindo.

Divine Mind in recovering the lost Light from the dark caves of its captors. And Agni, the God who befriends the other Gods by carrying to them the offerings of man in the Sacrifice and preparing the field here on earth for their manifestation, says the seer, is the original Flame of whom the Angirasas are the off-shoots. He it is who by the force of his Will and Knowledge—he is a seer, *rsi*—makes it possible for Indra to appear, undertake and lead to a successful culmination the battle for the Light. And the Maruts, the awakened powers of subtle life and thought are brought into being in the wake of the functioning of Agni, the burning of the Flame of the Seer-Will. They are roused and released from the torpidity in which they are normally submerged, and set into action. They partake of both the elements, the light of knowledge and the force of action of Agni; hence it is his greatness, his glory that they blazon when they manifest.[1] Not only they, but their weapons also are bright, their spears luminous because they are activated by a common energism raised to a white-heat of self-transcending power. The purified force of life that constitutes the substance of their being is charged with the luminous glow of the governing knowledge, *vidmanā*, the knowledge with which these *seers* proceed to work. Hence their form, their robe, their weapons, are all shining[2] and effective. "No half-

---

[1] *vrātam vrātam gaṇam gaṇam suśastibiragneḥ......gantāro yajnam* |

Host upon host, troop upon troop with their proclaimings of the Fire......they come (Rv. III. 26.6). Tr. by Sri Aurobindo.

[2] *ye anjiṣu ye vāśisu svabhānavaḥ srakṣu rukmeṣu svādiṣu śrāyā ratheṣu dhanvasu* |

They who shine self-luminous in decorations, in arms, in wreaths, in cuirass, in chariots, in bows. (Rv. V. 53.4)

lights, no impotent things are they, but mighty in aggression and puissant to attain. Spears of light they hold and they loose them from their hands at the children of Darkness; the flashing lightnings of the Thought-gods search the night and the light of heaven rises of itself on our souls at their battle-call." (Sri Aurobindo).

They move in chariots and these are drawn, significantly, by antelopes, the deer that fleet unmatched. This is how Rishi Kanva describes the legions of the Hosts:

Who, with spotted deer, with weapons and revealing cries, are self-luminous.[1]

Each of the Gods has his own characteristic vehicle, *v¯hana*; and the deer, the antelope, are the recognised carriers of the Maruts. These swift-footed animals represent the rapidly moving forces, on the plane of life, who speed the gods on their mission. Speed is their main feature. We must not fail to note the other epithets also that are used, each with a significance of its own. Sri Kapali Sastriar notes in his commentary:

"The antelopes celebrated for their storm-wind rush carry the host of the Maruts who are themselves born of the life-region and who endow the thought-movements with a divine velocity. The seeings, *ṛṣṭayaḥ*, (*ṛṣaterdarśanārthāt*) are weapons by reason of their piercing character. Of the Maruts of tempestuous speed, the very seeings become the weapons of aggression. Revealing, *anjibhiḥ*, is to be taken in apposition with *vāśibhiḥ*, words, cries. The words, the speeches, arise out of the violent rush of the Maruts, break open and reveal to sight or illumine things that are deep-seated or con-

[1] *ye pṛṣatibhiḥ ṛṣṭibhiḥ sākam vāśībhiranjibhiḥ* |
ajāyanta svabhānavaḥ || (Rv. I. 37.2)

cealed. Thus have the Maruts manifested themselves to the Rishi in Yajna, Sacrifice, with their *revealing cries* and full of the rays of the Light of Consciousness appropriate to their nature."[1]

To take another Rik describing the antelopes of the Maruts.

Ye to your chariot have yoked the spotted deer close; *the red one between them draws*.[2]

Here we must note the drawers of the carriage are mentioned as three in number, obviously to correspond to the three principles or levels of the being of man, viz. the body, the life and the mind. These Powers of upward movement, the Maruts, need the support of the energies of all the three parts of the being to proceed on their eventful journey. Of these three, says the Rishi, the middle one, the one of red hue takes the lead and thrusts forward; there can be no mistaking that this *rohita*, the *red* antelope, signifies a figure of the life-force embodying the power of action and enjoyment. It is this *vāhana* of life-energy laden with a special stress of the force of effectuation and joy that plays a pre-eminent role in speeding the car of the Maruts, with its compeers of the other two planes on either side to aid it.[3]

Thus equipped the Maruts arrive in their phalanx.

Like Agni with flashing splendour, gold-breasted, like tempest-blasts, self-moving, swift to lend their aid;

---

[1] Rig Veda Bhashya

[2] *upo ratheṣu pṛṣatīrayugdhvam pṛṣṭirvahati rohitaḥ* |
(Rv. I. 39.6)

[3] *Vide* Rig Veda Bhashya

As best of all foreknowers, excellent to guide, like Somas, delight-giving[1] *to him who follows the Law.*[2]

Note the epithets signifying their brilliance of form, their protective armour of gold[3], their spontaneities and swiftnesses, their vision and their knowledge and their outpourings of joy. Note also that their benevolence is only for those who go by the Rita, the Law of Truth.

The Maruts are they

Who move the mountains, scoff at the sea of waters.[4]

In the Vedic thought the mountain, the rock, symbolises the physical body, the material frame, inert and hard of structure, in whose caves of the nether regions of subconscience and inconscience lie coiled and asleep energies of various potentialities, rays of the light of consciousness awaiting their liberation. The Maruts, the dynamic powers that have begun their work in man, shake this mountain out of its torpor, strike at the hold of immobility and initiate a general movement of awakening and activity within the body. They bring about a release of the latent powers of knowledge and action. They scoff at the sea of waters. The wide expanse of the ocean signifies the

---

[1] Or, good to guard.

[2] *agnirna ye bhrājasā rukmavakṣaso vātāso na svayujaḥ sadya-ūtayaḥ |*
prajnātāro na jyeṣṭhāḥ sūnītayaḥ suśarmāṇo na somā ṛtam yate || (Rv. X. 78.2)

[3] "Gold is the concrete symbol of the higher light, the god of the Truth". (Sri Aurobindo).

The Maruts are also described as gold-helmeted, *hiraṇya-śiprāḥ*; tiaras wrought of gold are laid upon their heads, *śiprāḥ śirṣasu vitatā hiraṇyayīḥ* (Rv. V. 54.11). That is, their summits are enveloped in the light of the Truth.

[4] *ya īkhayanti parvatān tiraḥ samudramarṇavam* | (Rv. I. 19.7)

Infinity of Existence on the bosom of whose waters lie manifest the many universes that constitute the creation. These waters are the reservoir of the riches of powers and substances that are essential for the building up of all life. The Maruts, the gods of speedy activity, set these waters in movement, *calanam*, as the commentator says—they do not let them stay in their placid somnolence but provoke them into movement, an everwidening movement of the waves—and make it possible for the dormant forces and potencies to emerge by themselves or ready to be churned out by the *tapasyā*, the inner discipline of the initiate.[1]

---

[1] The amount of speculation into which the western scholars have been led by a Rik of this kind is indeed amusing. As it is rather typical of the manner in which they draw inferences, construct history and geography and pass verdict on the men and times of the Vedas, on data whose slenderness is matched only by the inadequacy of their own understanding, we reproduce extracts from the copious remarks of Max Muller on this Rik:

" Wilson remarks that the influence of the winds upon the sea, alluded to in this and the following verse, indicates more familiarity with the ocean than we should have expected from the traditional inland position of the early Hindus, and it has therefore been supposed by others that, even in passages like our own, *samudra* was meant for the sky, the waters above the firmament. But although there are passages in the Rig Veda where *samudra* must be taken to mean the welkin, this word shows in by far the larger number of passages the clear meaning of ocean.

"There is one famous passage (VII.95.2) which proves that the Vedic poets, who were supposed to have known the upper courses only of the rivers of the Penjab, had followed the greatest and most sacred of their rivers, the Sarasvati, as far as the Indian ocean. It is well known that, as early as the composition of the laws of the Manavas, and possibly as early as the composition of the Sutras on which these metrical laws are based, the river Sarasvati had changed its course, and that the place where that river disappeared underground was called Vinasana, the loss. This Vinasana forms, according

They do not merely shake but go further to effectuate their Power more definitively. Listen to Rishi Gotama:

With their ruddy tawny coursers which speed their chariot on, they come to the excellent Waters for glory. Brilliant like gold is the host with thunder. Earth they smite with the chariot's wheeling.[1]

Luminous alike in their form and their raiment, the Maruts arrive in their carriage sped by their steeds. The

---

to the laws of the Manavas, the western frontier of Madhyadeśa, the eastern frontier being formed by the confluence of the Ganga and Yamuna......

"It is very curious that while in the later Sanskrit literature the disappearance of the Sarasvati in the desert is a fact familiar to every writer, no mention of it should occur during the whole of the Vedic period, and it is still more curious that in one of the hymns of the Rig Veda (VII.95. 1-2) we should have a distinct statement that the Sarasvati fell into the sea......

"Though it may not be possible to determine by geological evidence the time of the changes which modified the southern area of the Penjab and caused the Sarasvati to disappear in the desert, still the fact remains that the loss of the Sarasvati is later than the Vedic age, and that at that time the waters of the Sarasvati reached the sea. Professor Wilson had observed long ago in reference to the rivers of that part of India, that there have been, no doubt, considerable changes here, both in the nomenclature and in the courses of the rivers, and this remark has been fully confirmed by later observations. I believe it can be proved that in the Vedic age the Sarasvati was a river as large as the Sutlej, that it was the last of the rivers of the Panjab, and therefore the iron gate, or the real frontier against the rest of India. At present the Sarasvati is so small a river that the epithets applied to the Sarasvatl in Veda have become quite inapplicable to it. Etc. Etc."

[1] *tèaruṇebhirvaramā piśangaiḥ śubhe kam yānti rathatūbhiraśvaiḥ rukmo na citraḥ svadhitivānpavyā rathasya janghananta bhūma* || (Rv. I. 88. 2.)

horses are described, significantly, to be of two colours. One kind is red hued, red signifying dynamic energy, intense activity. The other is tawny, the colour which stands for auspiciousness, a presaging of happiness. They come to the Waters, the excellent streams of the illumined Consciousness-Force in order to rain them on the thirsty soul of the worshipper and thus fulfil a glorious task. They strike the Earth: the wheels of their chariot, i.e., the pressure of their movement furrows the hard soil of the dense physicality of the being of the Yajamana. The physical body—which is signified by Earth—is inert, immobile and resistant to change. The mystics of the Veda frequently refer to the action of the gods[1] in beating down its resistance, in kneeding it into a sufficient malleability so that it could acquire the necessary plasticity and shape to receive and *hold* the riches of the higher light and power, which is indispensable if the Journey is to proceed smoothly without delay or breakdown. The Maruts, with their double pressure of force and light, work on the body in the very act of their ceaseless movement and make its ploughed soil ready to receive the seeds in the gift of the higher gods.[2]

They who set forth, glistening; *like wives*; *swift racers, sons of Rudra, doers of happy deeds*;

For the Maruts have made the Heaven and Earth to increase and grow; *heroes, they who grind small, in sacrifices they delight.*[3]

---

[1] E.g. Indra's working with his Vajra (I.28.1) Maruts (V·52.9) etc.

[2] *Vide* Sri T. V. Kapali Sastriar: *Rig Veda Bhāṣya*

[3] *pra ye śumbhante janayo na saptáyo yāmanrudrasya sūnavaḥ sudamsasaḥ* |
rodasī ha marutascakrire vṛdhe madanti virā vidatheṣu ghṛṣvayaḥ (Rv. I. 85.1)

The Maruts when they are awakened and well set in their career of movement, are bright with the fresh fervour of energy and the luminous glow of a higher knowledge. They are endearing to the worshipper like a beloved to her husband, wedded to the weal of him who sustains them with his aspiration, prayers and self-offering. They are known for the speed with which they run their course of accomplishment undeterred by any obstacles with which the path may be strewn; holding in themselves the guiding light of knowledge and the executing might of power, these sons of the God of Wrath, Rudra the Terrible, force their way with a divine fury that scorns and puts behind all the opposing forces on the Journey. But, for all their vehemence and impetuousness, the seer adds, they fulfil tasks that are happy, benign in their results—for gods and for man. For, the Rishi declares, the Maruts have formed the Heaven and the Earth in the Yajamana. In the symbolism of the Vedic mystics the Heaven and the Earth stand for the Higher Consciousness of the Mind and the awakened Consciousness in the Physical. The Maruts, i.e., the gods of the purified Thought-energies,[1] work to bring about the dawn and settling of the Higher Consciousness on the levels of the Mind on one hand, and on the other, extend and heighten the awakening of Consciousness in the physical being. They do not merely make the formation possible; they feed the Heaven and Earth with their own energisms and make them grow, enlarge their sway in their respective spheres in the expanding being of the worshipper.

And they *grind*, they grind small. These Powers are tireless in their work of breaking down the hard core of resistance to change offered by the materiality of the

---

[1] *pūtadakṣasaḥ* (Rv. VIII. 94.7.10)

physical body; the speed and violence for which they are renowned are not enough to achieve this purpose. They have to be incessantly at the task, laboriously bore through the Rock of Inconscience in which the body is rooted and heroes as they are, this too the Maruts accomplish. Charged with the dynamis of Life-Force, illumined by the Light of the Higher Mind, these powers of Aspiration in man are ever at work to eliminate the dogging inertia, immobility and tamasic unwillingness to change. The Sacrifices, the inner Yajna, to which the worshipper invokes the Higher Gods of Knowledge and Bliss to possess his being that is lovingly surrendered to them, hold a perennial attraction for them; because there in the advent of the greater godheads they achieve their own fuller perfection for the ultimate benefit of the Yajamana. Also, it is in the Sacrifices that the Yajamana offers the delectable sap of his own life-experiences and realisations to the Gods and the Maruts love their own share on which they thrive and increase.

Praise the unslayable host of the Maruts at play amidst radiances. It strengthened as it drank the sap.[1]

Rishi Kanva recalls the happy occasion when the Maruts arrived at a session of his Yajna. Encircled with the halo of their luminous rays, the host of the Maruts displayed themselves playful; nothing was beyond them; they could do things without effort because theirs is the might which knows no diminution. And strong as they were when they arrived, they augmented their strength, they grew in stature as they quaffed the sap, the Soma, the essence of Rishi's life-offering. The Maruts, like

---

[1] *pra śamsā goṣvaghnyam krīḷam yacchardho mārutam |*
jambhe rasasya vāvṛdhe || (Rv I. 37.5)

other Gods in the Veda, it must be noted, utilise this increase of strength, the exhilaration brought about by the enjoyment of the soulful offering, to the advantage of the offerer. They grow *in* and *for* him. They proceed to effect certain developments of an essential character in his Yajna.

Drink jrom the Purifier's vase in season, O Maruts Bountiful, sanctify the rite; for (it) ye are known.[1]

It is not enough for the Yajamana to make the offering of Soma. He must do it at the appropriate moment. Each of the Gods responds and accepts the Drink only when his appropriate time has arrived, i.e., when his separate and several requirements by way of equipment in the Sadhana of the mystic are met. Otherwise the effort is barren. The Rishi calls upon the bounteous Maruts to accept his offering at the right time; if in his eagerness he hastens the offering prematurely, it will be useless. They know the proper moment when they can fruitfully receive the Drink which is ready, purified, in the Cup of the being. And by so doing, the Maruts will consecrate the entre rite; they would be uplifting the Yajna to a still higher level of purification where all blemish is eliminated. Themselves purifying energies,[2] now sustained and nourished by the elixir of Soma-delight, the Maruts spread themselves rapidly and cover the whole Rite in a wide movement of purification and render it sanctified, thus entitling it to move further on its Journey to the Home of the Gods. The Maruts are well known for this beneficence and as such does the Rishi entreat them.

---

[1] *marutaḥ pibata ṛtunā potrādyajnam punītana |*
yūyam hi ṣṭhā sūdānavaḥ || (Rv. I. 15.2)

[1] *pāvakāḥ pāvakāsaḥ*

Or again,

They with their vigorous strength pushed the well up on high and clove asunder even the rock passing strong.

The Maruts, bounteous givers, blowing their pipe, in the exhilaration of Soma wrought their glorious deeds.[1]

Riding on the crest of an outburst of strength and joy caused by a fresh intake of the delightful Soma the Maruts performed deeds of valour and glory. Happy in the bubbling strength of execution of their purpose, happy with the thought of winning a bounty for their worshipper soon, they were blowing on their pipes; their joy found a natural expression in notes of music to the accompaniment of which they proceeded to work. And what did they do? They pushed the Waters of the well up from the depths, by their own unaided strength. Deep below in the confines of the subconscious and unconscious regions in the physical body of man there lie the Waters of Consciousness-Energy, the currents of light and power. It is due to the pressure of these elements, however much concealed from view in the somnolence of the apparent unconsciousness which characterises physical matter, that there is in creation an urge to advance, there is an out-flowering of more and more consciousness, a purpose observable even in the most mechanical movements of Nature. If the upward progress in the scale of life is to be speeded up, if the being of man is to advance towards fulfilment, it is indispensable that these principles are made more and more active, made to inform and govern

---

[1] *ūrdhvam nunudrevatam ta ojasā dādṛhāṇam cidbibhidurvi parvatam* |
dhamanto vāṇam marutaḥ sudānavo made somasya raṇyāni cakrire || (Rv. I. 85.10)

the movements of life and mind. And it is precisely this that the Maruts do in the seeker in their charge. They—the gods of forward movement incessantly at work in the being of man who is awakened—lift up these streams of Consciousness-Energy to the level of the Prana and then to that of Mind. That is to say, the activities of the life-force and the thought-force are more and more charged with the light and power of this Secret Principle. The well is lifted up from its nether base and its pristine Waters rendered available to the soul of the Yajamana on his arduous journey. No more for him is the acute thirst of want; the denying factors of ignorance, incapacity and limitation are progressively replaced by an increasing knowledge, power and freedom. But it is not easy to effect the change. There is the hard Rock of the dense layers of physical matter and unconsciousness which obstruct the flow of the Waters upwards. No human will and endeavour could break through this barrier unaided. The Maruts dynamite this solid Rock and clear the way for the surge of the leavening Waters.

Powerful by themselves, the Maruts are led in battle by One yet more powerful. The host of the Maruts has Indra at its head, *indrajyeṣṭhā marudgaṇāḥ*.[1] The Maruts are described as the brothers of Indra,[2] as his playmates,[3] as his army.[4] They pool their strengths at the disposal of Indra in his fight with the Arch-Enemy Vritra[5] who

---

[1] Rv. I. 23.8

[2] *indra......brātaro marutastava* (Rv. I. 170.2)

[3] *indrasya vai marutaḥ krīḍinaḥ* (Kaushitaki Br. 5.5 Gopatha 1.23)

[4] *indrasya vaī marutaḥ* (Kaushitaki Br. 5.4.5)

[5] *marutā ha vai krīdino vritram haniṣyantamindram āgatam tamabhitaḥ paricikrīḍurmahayantaḥ* |
(Shatapatha Br. 2.5.3.20)

obstructs the flow of the Waters. They come in their legions and support and follow him in his expedition to find and release the Ray-Cows imprisoned in the dark caves of the Captors.

Read in the symbology of the Vedic mystics, these descriptions not only stand naturally and perfectly explained but point to a profounder truth in the inner life of man and the universe. The Maruts are, as we have seen, the aspiring Though-Forces energised by the dynamism of purified life-energy. They are constantly striving to reach and spread themselves on the higher and yet higher reaches of mind till they arrive at the levels of the Pure Mind whose Lord is Indra. It is then they are said to be born again.[1] "The Maruts take our animal consciousness made up of the impulses of the nervous mentality, possess these impulses with their illuminations and drive them up the hill of being towards the world of Swar and the truths of Indra." (Sri Aurobindo). Already purified and subtilised sufficiently enough to gain entrance into this region of Svar, they find a natural release, a happy culmination, into the hands of the Lord of the luminous heavens of the Divine Mind. They find in him their archetype, the One in whose image they have been getting shaped; him they accept and follow as their First on the path of the Sacrifice-Journey. Naturally, if they gain a new status and stamp of a still Higher Consciousness by their following and being accepted by Indra, this Power of the Divine Mind also gains an increasing strength and mobility by their association and is thereby enabled to further the

---

[1] *ādaha svadhāmanu punargarbhatvamenire |*
dadhānā nāma yajniyam ||

And again after their self-law they have come to embryonic birth holding the sacrificial name. (Rv. I.6.4.) Tr. by Sri Aurobindo.

manifestation of the Higher Consciousness reigning above the triple world of Ignorance. On the harmony of this mutually enriching association and cooperation between the Maruts and Indra depends the progress[1] of the inner Yajna beyond the frontiers of the human mind. Indeed there are passages in the Rig Veda which describe the disharmony, even a conflict at times between the gods of the thought-forces and the God of the Divine Mind in the being of the worshipper and the unhappy consequences that ensue. But that is a subject in itself and cannot be dealt with adequately within the limits we have set for ourselves here. It is enough for our purpose to note that if the Maruts, the Thought-powers attempt to force their advance direct to their goal, bypassing and ignoring the Power of the Divine Intelligence in manifestation, that is to say, if the seeker on the Path to Immortality endeavours to shoot direct by sheer thought-force without a prior and proper fulfilment in the Truth of the Pure Mind, then there is an opposition from the Universal Power presiding over the "realm of pure intelligence through which the ascending soul passes into the divine Truth,"[2] and a consequent disharmony and arrest of progress.

The proper role of the Maruts is to so activise the being of man generally and specially the thought-being supported by *prāṇa*, to so subject the movements of mind and subtilised life to a ceaseless pressure of aspiration, rectification, purification, that they all, gradually, orient themselves and converge towards the highest heights of the mental skies where Indra, the Lord of Swar, is as it were, waiting for the aspiring soul. There the Maruts

---

[1] *marutvān no bhavatvindra ūti*, may Indra become associated with the Maruts for our thriving (Refrain in I. 100) Tr. by Sri Aurobindo.

[2] Sri Aurobindo.

have to deliver their charge and line up themselves behind the Premier One. Thus does Indra give his injunction to the Maruts:

"Giving the energy of your breath to their thoughts of varied light, become in them impellers to the knowledge of my truths. Whensoever the doer becomes active for the work and the intelligence of the thinker creates us in him, O Maruts, move surely towards that illumined seer."[1]

It is he, the Lord of Thoughts, *vṛṣsabho matīnām*, who is to take up the processed thought-movements and give them their fulfilling completeness; confirm them in the status proper to his own realm of divine illumination and once they are thus ready, to proceed to win for man the undying Light of the Sun of Truth.

In spite of his unequalled prowess Indra does not act alone. He is joined by the Maruts who have arrived, he is increased in his strength by the strength of their legions. By their instrumentation he effects and extends his sway over the domain of men. Thus is Indra entreated by the Rishi to accept the sacrifice, accept the aid of the toiling Maruts, so that by them increased he can affirm himself (in the being of the Rishi) with a fuller pervasiveness and by him protected they can fulfil themselves, their brilliances and their mights, *in the ordered method of Truth, ṛtuthā.*

Thou by whom the movements of the mind grow conscient and brilliant in our mornings through the bright power of the

---

[1] *manmāni citrā apivātayanta eṣām bhūta navedā ma ṛtānām* |
ā yad duvasyād duvase na kārurasmāncakre mānyasya medhā |
oh ṣu varta maruto vipramaccha | (Rv. I. 165.13.14)
Tr. by Sri Aurobindo.

continuous Dawns, O Bull of the herd, establish by the Maruts inspired knowledge in us,—by them in their energy thou energetic, steadfast, a giver of might. Do thou, O Indra, protect the Powers in their increased might; put away thy wrath against the Maruts, by them in thy forcefulness upheld, who have right perceptions. May we find the strong impulsion that shall break swiftly through."[1]

To quote the luminous commentary of Sri Aurobindo on these Riks:

"The Maruts represent the progressive illumination of human mentality, until from the first obscure movements of mind which only just emerge out of the darkness of the subconscient, they are transformed into an image of the luminous consciousness of which Indra is the Purusha, the representative Being. Obscure, they become conscient; twilit, half-lit or turned into misleading reflections, they surmount these deficiencies and put on the divine brilliance. This great evolution is effected in Time gradually, in the mornings of the human spirit, by the unbroken succession of the Dawns. For Dawn in the Veda is the goddess symbolic of new openings of divine illumination on man's physical consciousness. She alternates with her sister Night; but that darkness itself is a mother of light and always Dawn comes to reveal what the black-browed Mother has prepared. Here, however, the seer seems to speak of continuous dawns, not broken by these intervals of apparent rest and obscurity. By the

---

[1] *yena mānasāścitayanta usrā vyuṣṭiṣu śavasā śaśvatīnām |*
sa no marudbhirvṛṣabha śravo ghā ugra ugrebhiḥ sthaviraḥ sahodāḥ ||
tvam pāhīndre sahīyaso nṛnbhavā marudbhiravayātaheḷaḥ |
supraketebhiḥ sāsahirdadhano vidyameṣam vṛjanam jīradānum || (Rv. I. 171.5-6) Tr. by Sri Aurobindo.

brilliant force of that continuity of successive illuminations the mentality of man ascends swiftly into fullest light. But always the force which has governed and made possible the transformation, is the puissance of Indra. It is that supreme Intelligence which through the Dawns, through the Maruts, has been pouring itself into the human being. Indra is the Bull of the radiant herd, the Master of the thought-energies, the Lord of the luminous dawns.

Now also let Indra use the Maruts as his instruments for the illumination. By them let him establish the supramental knowledge of the seer. By their energy his energy will be supported in the human nature and he will give that nature his divine firmness, his divine force, so that it may not stumble under the shock or fail to contain the vaster play of puissant activities too great for our ordinary capacity.

The Maruts, thus reinforced in strength, will always need the guidance and protection of the superior Power. They are the Purushas of the separate thought-energies, Indra the one Purusha of all thought-energy. In him they find their fullness and their harmony. Let there then be no longer strife and disagreement between this whole and these parts. The Maruts, accepting Indra, will receive from him the right perception of the things that have to be known. They will not be misled by the brilliance of a partial light or carried too far by the absorption of a limited energy. They will be able to sustain the action of Indra as he puts forth his force against all that may yet stand between the soul and its consummation.

So in the harmony of these divine Powers and their aspirations may humanity find that impulsion which shall be strong enough to break through the myriad oppositions of this world and, in the individual with his composite personality or in the race, pass rapidly on towards the goal so constantly glimpsed but so distant even to him who seems to himself almost to have attained."

The Maruts are also associated with another major God of the Veda, Agni. In many of the Riks Agni is called upon to come to the Sacrifice along with the host of the Maruts and in some Agni is even described as bringing the Maruts to birth. Theirs is the glory of Fire, declares Vishwamitra.[1] We do not of course take serious notice of the puerile explanation of the matter by western scholars whose position is so admirably summed by Wilson in one sentence: "(The association) is an obvious metaphor expressing the action of wind upon fire." It is clear from our study thus far of the inner, the psychological character of the Maruts, that this relation is only natural. For, Agni the first of the Gods to be born in the mortals, is in his first manifestation the flaming force of aspiration and self-effectuating seer-will. In his working, *vrata,* as the being of man in its totality gets more and more warmed up and heated with a consuming passion for the eradication from itself of the triple noose of the lower self and for a rapid transcendence into a life governed by and growing in the Higher Truth and its Law, there are awakened and released into action the powers of might and speed charged with a soaring aspiration who breaking forth from the domain of nervous vitality lead up to the regions of Thought and carry everything before them in their wide and onward movement. Thus describes Rishi Parashara:

When a flame of energy came to this King of men for impelling force, when in their meeting Heaven was cast in him like a

[1] *agniśriyo marutaḥ* (Rv. III. 26.5)

pure seed, the Fire gave birth to a host, young and faultless and perfect in thought and sped it on its way.[1]

Agni is the ruling Deity of Earth. Whether externally as the elemental fire, the principle of heat and light which keeps life going or on the esoteric side as the divine Flame which manifests in the heart of creatures and urges them forward, Agni is the Lord who leads man, the son of Earth. Like a king to his subjects, he tends to the needs of those in whom he is awakened, intercedes on their behalf with the other Gods, carries their offerings to the destination. He forms the bridge for man to ascend from Earth to Heaven and Beyond. When this Agni, recalls the seer, was activated by a burst of energy his pace quickened, impelled by the increasing drive within, and he hastened towards the heights of the Heaven of the Pure Mind carrying with him the best in the worshipper. There arrived, Agni receives (for man) the first touch, the pregnant touch of that Higher Consciousness and immediately, as a direct consequence of this inflow of the pure and illumined mental substance, he is able to charge and set afire the entire Thought-region in man. The multitude of thought-forces are uplifted and galvanised into their churning and striving movement. The host of the Maruts is born. Drawing their power and mobility from the purified, inexhaustible life-energies at their base, they are young and fresh; open and aspiring to the flow of the currents of the pure Intelligence above, they are right-thoughted and right-functioning, above the bounds of ignorance and error in which the human mind normally moves. Agni not only gives the generating touch but gives also a push

---

[1] *ā yadiṣe nṛpatim teja ānat śuci reto niṣiktam dyaurabhīke | agniḥ sardhamanavadyam yuvānam svādhyam janayatsūdayacca* || (Rv. I. 71.8) Tr. by Sri Aurobindo.

and velocity which speed them on their career as fire-tongued increasers of Truth.[1]

The Path of the Maruts is trailed by a blaze of light. The Maruts are spoken of as harbingers of light and that is only proper for these thought-energies are powers that seek and make for higher knowledge. As we have seen, they are always on the move for attaining the consciousness of the higher and still higher summits of the Mind and they arrive at their full maturity when they are accepted on the levels of luminous mentality and they grow into the status of the Consciousness native to that plane. Thus they are always instinct with a charge of Knowledge growing into greater Knowledge. And Knowledge, as we know, is symbolised in the Veda by the living figure of Light. It is this Light of Knowledge that follows in their wake, *radiance streams along their paths*[2], says the Rishi.

After the Maruts followed close, of its own accord, the splendour of Heaven[3]...

The Maruts do not have to make any special effort to bring the Light; the splendour of the Heavens of illumined mental consciousness follows them naturally, of its own accord, because they have grown into it and are now become so many centres of manifestation or emanations of that Consciousness whose form is Light.

Or,

---

[1] *agnijihvā ṛtāvṛdhaḥ* (Rv. I. 44.14)

[2] *vartmāni eṣām anriyate ghṛtam* | (Rv. I. 85.3)

[3] *anvenām vaha......maruto......bhānurarta tmanā divaḥ* | (Rv. V. 52.6)

Conceal the concealed darkness; repel every devourer. Create the Light for which we long.[1]

It is within the experience of every seeker on the mystic Path that there is somewhere in his own being a core of obscurity, a part that does not follow and keep pace with the other parts in their growth towards light, knowledge and freedom. It is given to the obstinate rule of inertia, shot through and through with opaque masses of unconsciousness and it not only opposes all infiltration of light in its own region, but casts its shadow on the rest of the being also. This is the darkness concealed to the outer view, lying embedded in the denser layers of the physical being. The Rishi, engaged in the Yajna of self-transcendence, doubtless is confronted with the challenge of this Darkness and prays to the dynamic Maruts to remove it from view, to eliminate it from the scene of action.

This done, there remains another difficulty. There are plenty of malevolent elements in Nature opposed to the progress of man—forces and beings operating on the physical as well as the supra-physical levels, trying to *eat up* what man has achieved in his endeavour. In his unguarded moments they lure him into movements of forgetfulness or sloth, or wrong-occupation, gain entry into his atmosphere and rob him of the spiritual wealth so far won. These are the Dasyus, the Rakshasas who infest the route of the Traveller, who, when they do not find sufficient opening in his armour for surreptitious entrance, do not hesitate to launch a frontal attack on his person at some stage or another. The Maruts with their piercing

---

[1] *gūhatā guhyam tamo vi yāta viśvamatrinam ||*
jyotiṣkartā yaduṣmasi || (Rv. I. 86.10)

sights and luminous strengths can be safely trusted to spot and deal with them. This is the second prayer of the Rishi.

And as a result of the successful accomplishment of the first two, the third and the most important. The clogging darkness has been removed; the eager enemy is kept at bay; the way is cleared for a decisive and consummating realisation: the advent and establishment of the Light, the Supreme Light for which the Rishi and his high-souled companions have been longing. The Maruts are the holders of the universal Light[1] and to them the Rishi prays to achieve this victory for him, to set in him this Light which once for all puts an end to the era of false lights and twilights and ensures an undeviating journey from knowledge to greater knowledge, from truth to higher truth.[2]

And finally, the Maruts are the Healers.

O Maruts, generous in gifts, bring us the medicaments that belong to your company.

Ye coursers who are friends to us.[3]

---

[1] *marutsu viśvabhānuṣu* (Rv. IV. 1.3)

[2] It is interesting to note that even Sayana has felt constrained to give the spiritual import of the Rik in his commentary, albeit as an alternative:

yadvā guhyam guhāyām śarirantargataguhārūpe hṛdaye bhavam tamobhāvarūpājnānam dūhata vināśayata | atriṇam puruṣarthasyāttāram kāmakrodhādhikam sarvam vinirgamayata | yattodjyotiḥ paratattvasākṣātkārarūpam jnānam kāmayāmahe prāṇapānādipancavṛthirūpā he marutaḥ tatkartā kurutā |

[3] *maruto mārutasya na ā bheṣajasya vahata sudānavaḥ yūyam sakhāyaḥ saptayaḥ* || (Rv. VIII. 20.23)

As sons of Rudra, the Physician of physicians,[1] the Maruts also have the healing touch, the knowledge of the Balm that soothes. They are ever on the move and they know and can draw upon the healing powers wherever they are—in the rivers of life, in the ocean of Consciousness-Energy or in the hilly tracts of the physical Substance.

Carry it to our bodies, ye who see all ; bless us graciously therewith.

End the malady, O Maruts ; make whole again the afflicted (frame) of the sick one.[2]

The Maruts know all the medicines and where they are to be found, says the Rishi and prays that they may bring them for the benefit not of himself alone, but of the community of seekers who are engaged in the Sacrifice. Whether as a result of overstrain or misdirected effort or hostile attacks from outside or from the *sin* of actions in disharmony with the call of the Truth to which he has centrally dedicated himself, the many-tiered being of the seeker is afflicted by malady ; it cannot function in its fullness. And as long as this imperfection and incapacity is allowed to continue, it is not possible to advance far on the Journey. The Maruts have the knowledge of the means wherewith to remove the ailment and the capacity

---

[1] *bhiṣaktamam bhiṣajām* (Rv. II. 33.4)
sahasram te bheṣajā thousand medicines of Rudra (Rv. VII. 463)
hastē bibrat beshaja carrying medicines in hand (Rv. I. 114.5)
kva sya te rudra mṛḷayākurhasto yo asti bheṣajo jalāṣaḥ |
Where. Oh Rudra, is thy joy-dispensing hand, the hand that healeth and delighteth ! (Rv. II. 33.7)

[2] *viśvam paśyanto vibhṛthā tanūṣvā tenā no adhi vocata* |
kṣamā rapo maruta āturasya na iṣkartā vihutam punaḥ ||
(Rv. VIII. 20.26)

to restore the health of the worshipper to a condition perfect in its all-round completeness, *make whole*, *iskarta*. Indeed, the Maruts are well-known for their pure, most wholesome and felicitous medicines from the time of Manu, the First Man.[1]

Be it noted that there are not the illnesses of the physical body alone. There are the ills of the mind, the afflictions of the life-being, the sicknesses of the soul. Those whose living is not confined to the normal life of the physical senses alone, know how real the effects of these maladies are. Indeed, for the seekers of the Spirit, for those whose lives are lived more and more on the subtler, the psychological and the yet deeper levels of being, the ills of want and limitation, ignorance and obscurity in the subtler bodies of life, mind and *antaḥkaraṇa*, the emotional, and what is more the disharmonies between the different parts of being, e.g., the outer and inner, the higher and lower, are much more galling and exasperating than the diseases of the body. The Maruts carry the medicine which acts on all of these and they pour it in torrents[2] on him in whom they are active. Their purified energies of Life-force, the illuminations of the higher Light with which their Thought-content is charged, the sweetnesses which they eternally carry in their person[3] and the currents of Bliss which are inalienable from the streams of Waters they release with the help of Indra, eliminate the defects of weakness, incapacity and incompleteness, displace the elements of ignorance, falsehood and error and lift the many-bodied

---

[1] *yā vo bheṣajā marutaḥ śucini yā śantamā vṛṣano yā mayobhū* | *yāni manuravṛṇitā pitā naḥ* || (Rv. II. 33.13)

[2] *vṛṣṭvī......bheṣajam......marutaḥ* (Rv. V. 53.14)

[3] *mādayiṣnavaḥ* (Atharva Veda, VII. 77·3)

being of the Yajamana out of the circle of struggle and suffering into the larger spaces of Peace and Happiness where corners are rounded, gaps are filled and harmony established in spontaneous movements of growth into Wholeness.

Such, then, was the character and import of the Maruts to the Vedic Initiate whatever they may have meant to the uninstructed. Such also is their significance —and value to us, if we will—if, in our study of the Hymns, we do not stop short with their external physiognomy and activities, but look deeper and awaken to the truth of their role in the life of every seeker of the Ideal of Immortality.

SACRIFICE IN THE VEDA

THE institution of Sacrifice has played an important part in almost all the ancient religions but its role in the way of life developed by the Vedic Aryans and continued by their descendants across the centuries has been something unique. To them Sacrifice is not simply a group festival; it has a significant place in the daily life of the individual too. It permeates the entire life of their society. Sacrifice has been recognised by them as a basic principle of existence establishing and maintaining relation between man and man, man and God. Thus calls an ancient Rishi of the Veda:

> *Sacrifice, O Adityas, is your inward monitor; be kind*
>
> *For in the bond of kindred we are bound to you,*[1]

declaring a truth which is echoed in the famous verse of Gita:

> *Foster by this (Sacrifice) the gods and let the gods foster you;*
>
> *Fostering each other you shall attain to the supreme good.*[2]

What is the origin, nature and significance of the Sacrifice? *Sacrifice in the Veda*[3] deals comprehensively with the subject of sacrifice—external sacrifice—in the age of the Rig Veda. We say *external* advisedly, for, the rite with which this book deals is only the exoteric

---

[1] *yajno hilo vo antara ādityā asti mṛlata |*
yuṣme iddho api ṣmasi sajātye || (Rv. VIII. 18.19)

[2] *devān bhāvayatānena te devā bhāvayantu vaḥ |*
parasparam bhāvayantaḥ śreyaḥ paramāvāpsyata || (III. 11)

[3] By K. R. Potdar. Publishers: Bharatiya Vidya Bhavan, Bombay.

aspect of the Sacrifice; there is much more behind it which it is indispensable to know if one is to grasp the real intention and full meaning of this central fact of Vedic worship—the Yajna. But to that we shall turn later.

Prof. Potdar approaches his subject with all the equipment of a scholar trained in the modern methods of research but with a mind that is not overawed by the 'authority' of the western Orientalists. Discussing the position of the Sacrifice in the Vedic society, its relation to the Hymns and to the Gods, in the first three chapters, he points out that many of these Indologists fail to note the gap between the age of the Rig Veda when ceremonial sacrifice was part—like the hymns—of the religion, and the times of the Brahmanas when it became a religion in itself. These scholars draw their inferences about Vedic sacrifice largely from and under the inspiration of the Brahmanic literature which is much posterior to the Rig Vedic period and out of consonance with its spirit. The author wisely relies upon the "evidence presented by the hymns themselves for we can say that the hymns themselves can act as an armour to guard the safety of the conclusions they themselves indicate."[1]

So also, he questions the view of some like Bloomfield[2] that the Mantras were composed for purposes of ritual. "In the composition of the hymns," he writes, "the dominant idea in the mind of the poet does not appear to be the employment at a particular sacrificial rite but rather the propitiation of the divinity." Which of them is of earlier origin, the Mantra or the Sacrifice? The

---

[1] *brahma varma mamāntaram* (Rv. VI. 75·19)

[2] Viz. "It is sacrifice to the gods, treated poetically. In other words, the poems are incidental to sacrifice."

author is inclined to rely upon the utterance of the Rishi "who though he may have been relatively late in the tradition of the hymns and the sacrifices, was certainly much nearer to them than the later speculators in the field of the interpretation of the Rig Veda.":

First the Gods brought the hymnal into being; then they engendered Agni, their oblation.

He was their sacrifice...[1]

Which of them was more important? Both the Mantras and the Sacrifice were means to a single end. "Using a metaphor, it can be said that in the days of the Rig Veda, the hymns and the sacrifice were the two horses, drawing the chariot of the propitiation of the divinities. In the days of the Brahmanas, with the shifting of the emphasis, the performance of the sacrificial rite has become a chariot to be drawn by the hymns and the divinities." Each complements the other. If "the hymns are said to be making the sacrifice divine,[2] it is also stated that the hymns shone at the place of sacrifice only.[3] The hymns in their basic aspect of speech in its divine form are said to be guarded in the place of sacrifice by the (seers)."[4]

The Riks leave no room for speculation regarding the relation between the Gods and the Sacrifice. They

---

[1] *sūktavākam prathamamadidagnimādiddhavirajanayanta devāḥ* | *sa yeṣām yajno abhavat tanūpaḥ*......(Rv. X. 88.8)

[2] *duṣṭaram yasya sāma cidṛdhagyajno na mānuṣaḥ* | (Rv. X. 93.8)

[3] *ṛtasya hi sadasah dhītiḥ adyant* | (Rv. X. 111.2)

[4] *patango vācam manasā bibharti tām gandharvovadgarbhe antaḥ* |
tām dyotamānām svaryam maniṣāmṛtasya padaye kavaye nipānti || (Rv. X. 177.2)

clearly announce: sacrifice is in the heart of the Gods;[1] the Gods have raised the sacrifice to a high level; sacrifice has to have the protection,[2] assistance,[3] the acceptance and confirmation of the Gods.[4] And what is more, sacrifice has been created by the Gods.[5] It is the ladder by which they ascended.[6] Of all the Gods, the position of Agni *vis a vis* the Sacrifice is the most outstanding. He is the leader, the vicar, the knower of sacrifices.[7] There are many other epithets emphasising his special relation to the sacrifice. There are indeed other Gods like Indra, Ashwins, etc., who hold important positions and whose presence is indispensable; yet the role of Agni is paramount. The author observes that the number of hymns devoted to the deities determines their position in the Vedic pantheon. We cannot agree. It is pertinent to recall what Sri Aurobindo notes in this connection: "The importance of the Gods has not to be measured by the number of hymns devoted to them or by the extent to which they are invoked in the thoughts of the Rishis, but by the functions which they perform. Agni and Indra to whom the majority of the Vedic hymns are addressed are not greater than Vishnu and Rudra, but the functions they fulfil in the internal and external world were the most active, dominant, directly effective for the psychological discipline of the ancient mystics. This alone is the

---

[1] *yajno hīḷo vo antaraḥ* | (Rv. VIII. 18.19)

[2] *tābhiḥ ūtibḥiḥ āgatam* | (Rv. I. 112.2)

[3] *kṛṇutam no adhvaram* | (Rv. I. 93.12)

[4] *devānām śamsamṛta ā ca* | (Rv. I. 141.11)

[5] *yajnam janitvī tanvī ni māmṛjuḥ* | (Rv. X. 65.7)

[6] *devānāmutkramaṇam* (Yajurveda. VI, 26)

[7] *advarasya praṇetā yajnanīḥ rathiḥ pratnaḥ hotā sa vedo yajnamānuṣak etc.*

reason of their predominance." Sri Kapali Sastriar points out: "The Sun, the glorious symbol of the Truth, the supreme Godhead of the Veda, referred to as That One, *tad ekam*, is addressed in fewer hymns than Indra or Agni or even Maruts. The Rishis invoke the powers of Agni and Indra because they are of constant and immediate consequence in the psychological and spiritual discipline of these mystics, and hence the importance and not because they are superior to the Sun; similarly Maruts, children of Rudra are not greater than their Father though there are more hymns addressed to them than to Rudra in the Rig Veda. The same may be said of Vishnu and Rudra to whom lesser number of hymns are devoted and yet Indra and Agni are not greater than they."[1]

We cannot subscribe either to the author's explanation when he says that the worship of more than one God in the Sacrifice was due to a desire to promote amity among the devotees of different divinities. Each godhead in the Veda has its special function for which it is brought into manifestation. And the invocation of a particular deity or deities related to the need of the worshipper in his personal life. At times and in certain stages it would be Agni whose help was specially called for and at others the Maruts and Indra or Mitra and Varuna and so on depending upon the nature of the want or wants felt by the seeker. But we anticipate what we have reserved to say later on.

The author proceeds to describe the scene of the Sacrifice, the importance of the altar, *Vedi*, the number of implements used, the various offerings that were made in the different types of Sacrifice. Attention is drawn to how

---

[1] *Vide* Further Lights: The Veda and the Tantra.

in spite of all the care and attention given to the ceremonial side of the ritual, the cardinal importance of the heart of the sacrifice, i.e., the spirit governing the performance, was not lost sight of. Thus he recalls an instance where lack of sincerity on the part of the sacrificer vitiated all the elaborate preparations made and God Indra would not respond.[1] He successfully contests the view of scholars like Macdonald who claim to have discovered traces of magic and sorcery in the rituals of the Rig Vedic Aryans. The Rishis of the Veda would vehemently scorn any suggestion to that effect, as indeed does Seer Vasishtha:

So may I die this day if I have harassed any man's life or if I be a fiend,

Yea, may he lose all his ten sons together who with false tongue hath called me Yatudhana.[2]

On the other hand, the seers of the Veda attached the highest importance to the Right, the Truth alone and pursued it as the only enduring value. Witness:

Facile to the conscious to distinguish the true and false: their words oppose each other. Of these two that which is true and honest, Soma protects and brings the false to nothing.[3]

Speaking of the conception of Sacrifice pervading the whole life in that age, the author points out how even death was elevated into a term of Sacrifice and thus

---

[1] Rv. V. 61·2.

[2] *adyā murīya yadi yātudhāno asmi yadi vāyustatapa pūruṣasya, adhā sa vīrairdeśabhirvi yūyā yo mā mogham yātudhānetyāha.*
(Rv. VII. 104.15)

(*Yātudhāna*, goblin or sorcerer.)

[3] *suvijñānam cikituṣe janāya saccāsacca vacasī paspṛdhāte, tayoryatsatyam yataradṛjiyastaditsomóvati hantyāsat.*
(Rv. VII. 14.12)

invested with special significance. The Veda records that Yama, the God of Death, was the first to offer his body to Death and that he did so as an offering in his Sacrifice for the weal of gods and men.[1]

The role of the different classes of Priests, the part played by the Patrons, the mystical element in the Sacrifice and the influence of the institution of Sacrifice on the social organism are some of the other main subjects dealt with systematically with a wealth of material from Vedic literature. The discussion is throughout learned, nowhere dogmatic.

The author observes in conclusion: "The overall impression of the sacrifice that we thus secure is of an idea which has been very ably conceived and developed for a pretty long stretch of time. Creation has been thought of in terms of the sacrifice; death is being looked upon in the light of the sacrifice; human life appears to be considered as permeated by the idea of the sacrifice. Sacrifice thus appears to have been considered as the very basis of life and it is for this reason that the Rita has come to be identified with the sacrifice." He notes in another place: "Sacrifice was considered to be a system of cosmic importance as it concerns the whole universe. Its creation is in line with that of the Heaven, Earth and Waters which symbolise the living world."

Truly said. But we would ask, can these remarks apply to Sacrifice as it has come to be generally known? If sacrifice means nothing more than a religious or socio-religious ritual and ceremony with a peculiar and propitiatory aim—albeit with a dash of exuberant sentiment —performed by a limited number of specially trained

[1] Rv. X 13·4

priests with the means provided by wealthy patrons, how could it be described as the "centre of the world", *bhuvanasya nābhiḥ*, the universal lodestar of life? How could it be associated with Rita—Truth—that transcends the bourne of Time and Space?

Obviously there is something more than what strikes the eye. The author seems to be aware of this aspect of the matter. Throughout his treatment of the subject he feels every now and then that there is in the Veda some significance, some sense which constantly shadows and peeps over the surface meaning. Thus for instance, speaking of the repeated mention of the figure seven in the Veda, he observes: "In the case of *sapta yavhiḥ, or sapta hotra* or *sapta hotrāṇi* and a number of things associated with the number seven, it appears that some mystical significance is attached to the figure seven......" Dealing with Hymns, *Nithas*, he says they are "referred to as secret speeches or words, may be on account of the low tone in which they were to be sung at the sacrifices or on account of some mystical significance that had come to be associated with them." Of offerings he writes: "With certain materials of sacrificial performance too, such mystical significance is associated. Their reference to prayers and the offerings indicates the association with sacrifice and...it is said of Soma that with the eyes of Soma the poet can see the *hiraṇyaya* ... Some mystical significance is associated with *ghṛta*, the mysterious source of strength of the *ghṛta*, which it possesses and transmits to the gods indicated by reference to its secret name, its being 'the tongue of the Gods' and 'the centre immortality'."

So too of sacrifice, he is aware of something mystic and observes:

"It can however be seen that a kind of mystical element has come to be associated with the sacrificial performance in its various aspects so as to lead it to the divinity with a sort of mysterious source of strength." He draws attention to the description of the Vedi, the altar which is the seat of sacrifice, as the farthest extremity of the earth, *paro antaḥ pṛthivyaḥ*,[1] as the nodus of Truth, *ṛtsya nābhih*.[2] He notes that in more places than one Sacrifice is referred to as an entity with a consciousness, *cetana*; itself conscious it awakens the Gods to conscious activity;[3] and the Gods themselves perform the *conscious* sacrifice, *cetanam yajñam*. And he adds: "Sacrifice would thus appear to stand as a symbol, a wheel for generating the power that was essential for the sustenance of the human society."

Is it possible to pass by the following Rik without feeling the presence of something mystic and symbolic about it?

The car, fresh and pure, is ready at dawn; four yokes it hath, three whips and reins seven.

Ten-wheeled, benevolent to man, winner of light, urged forward with impulsions and thoughts.[4]

What then is the real significance of the Yajna which is likened by the mystics of the Veda to a thread, *tantu*,

---

[1] Rv. I. 164.35

[2] Rv. X. 13.3

[3] *tatrāmṛtasya cetanam yajnam te tanavavahai* (Rv. I. 170.4)

[4] *prātā ratho navo yoji sasniścaturyugastrikaśaḥ saptaraśmiḥ daśāritro manuṣyaḥ svarṣāḥ sa iṣṭibhirmatibhī ramhyo bhūt.* (Rv. II. 18.1)

to a boat, *nau*, to Manu himself,[1] to a carriage, *ratha*, whose horses are the hymns and the charioteer Agni? What is this Yajna through which, the Yajur Veda declares, the ritual of Yajna prospers?[2]

The Yajna, Sacrifice, in the Veda is of course the ritual that goes by the name. But that is not the whole of the matter. Behind the external ceremony there lies a deeper truth which is the soul that gives life to the rite. The outer ritual is the garb, the symbol of an inner Yajna, a self-consecration by which the Vedic worshipper offers all that he is and has to the higher Powers, the divinities, and lays himself in their benevolent hands which lift him upto their Beatitude. In the words of Sri Aurobindo:

"The elements of the outer sacrifice in the Veda are used as symbols of the inner sacrifice and self-offering; we give what we are and what we have in order that the riches of the divine Truth and Light may descend into our life and become the elements of our inner birth into the Truth,—a right thinking, a right understanding, a right action must develop in us which is the thinking, impulsion and action of that higher Truth, *ṛtasya preṣa*, *ṛtasya dhīti*, and by this we must build ourselves in that Truth. Our sacrifice is a journey, a pilgrimage and a battle,—a travel towards the Gods and we also make that

---

[1] "*yajño manuḥ pramatirṇaḥ pitā*; the metaphor indicates the importance of the sacrifice even for the origination of the human race. The suggestion of cosmic importance associated with the sacrifice indicates the importance of the sacrifice for the general understanding of the problem of human life in all its aspects."

[2] *yajno yajnena kalpatam* (Yv. IX. VS. 21.)

journey with Agni, the inner Flame as our path-finder and leader.'[1]

"The image of this sacrifice is sometimes that of a journey or voyage; for it travels, it ascends; it has a goal — the vastness, the true existence, the light, the felicity —and it is called upon to discover and keep to the good, the straight and the happy path to the goal, the arduous yet joyful road of the Truth. It has to climb led by the flaming strength of the divine will, from plateau to plateau as of a mountain, it has to cross as in a ship the waters of existence, traverse its rivers, overcome their deep pits and rapid currents; its aim is to arrive at the far-off ocean of light and infinity."[2]

"The Vedic deities are names, powers, personalities of the universal Godhead and they represent each some essential puissance of the Divine Being. They manifest the cosmos and are manifest in it. Children of Light, Sons of the Infinite, they recognise in the soul of man their brother and ally and desire to help and increase him by themselves increasing in him so as to possess his world with their light, strength and beauty. The Gods call man to a divine companionship and alliance; they attract and uplift him to their luminous fraternity, invite his aid and offer theirs against the Sons of Darkness and Division. Man in return calls the Gods to his sacrifice, offers to them his swiftnesses and his strengths, his clarities and his sweetnesses,—milk and butter of the shining Cow, distilled juices of the Plant of Joy, the Horse of the Sacrifice, the cake and the wine, the grain for the God-Mind's radiant coursers. He receives them into his being

[1] *Hymns to the Mystic Fire.*

[2] *On the Veda.*

and their gifts into his life, increases them by the hymns and the wine, and forms perfectly,—as a smith forges iron, says the Veda—their great and luminous godheads."[1]

Studied with this background and in the light of this esoteric interpretation revived by Sri Aurobindo, we find that everything connected with the Sacrifice has a symbolic meaning. The implements used, the offerings made, the gifts showered and even the gods that are invoked signify and stand for certain deeper verities in the life of the seeker of the Life Beatific.

---

[1] *On the Veda.*

VRATYAKANDA IN THE ATHARVA VEDA

THOUGH the Indian Vedic literature as a whole has been treated by the western scholars as a kind of juvenile expression of the primitive society of Nature-worshipping Aryans, there are certain parts, notably in the Rig Veda, which have been singled out with a touch of exuberant condescension as pieces of rare philosophical value. May be they are later accretions; may be also they are ideas which floated down from further West; all the same they are gems of poetic beauty and daring quest. So too there are elevating portions in the Sama and the Yajur Veda. But none—almost none—in the Atharva. The Atharva Samhita is simply and plainly a treatise of charms, magic, witchcraft and spurious medicine. It is a collection concocted by the later wily Brahmans, overspread by liberal helpings from the Rik and Yajus Samhitas, and tagged on to the three real Vedas, *Trayi*, with a view to fortify and perpetuate their own priestly hold on the growing society. Or possibly, say some scholars, the hymns of the Atharva represent the life and movement of the lower strata of the society as the Rig Veda does of the higher classes.

The author of *The Atharva Veda*: *Vrātyakāṇḍa* rejects this consistent condemnation of the Atharva Veda by the Orientalists. In a spirited Introduction he questions their premisses and exposes the weakness of their argument He writes:

"There are prayers for freedom from various diseases and relief from pain and many of these prayers are meant

---

By Sri Sampurnanand. Publishers: Ganesh & Co., Madras 17.

to accompany the administration of suitable medical treatment, internal and external. There are references to a number of herbs possessing valuable medicinal properties and such a non-spiritual subject as the catheter also finds mention. There are also no doubt the portions dealing with *Yatus* and other spirits of the dark worlds. But while the Atharva Samhita no doubt contains a proportionately large amount of such matter, it does not stand alone. There are references to such spirits elsewhere as well, particularly in the Rig Veda and even charms and incantations are not an exclusive feature of the Atharva Veda...The Gods to whom the prayers are addressed are the same as those who are sought to be approached through the most sublime of Vedic prayers. They give expression to the hopes, aspirations and fears of the common man who yearns for a place in the everlasting regions of the gods but cannot, at the same time, forget his crops and cattle, his wife in the pains of labour, his friends and his enemies. The man who gives thought to such matters is not necessarily a pessimist or a victim of superstition. The fact that he fortifies his dose of secular medicine with a prayer gives evidence of shrewd commonsense, not of a mind dulled by the teachings of a priestly hierarchy. In conjunction with the Mantras in this and other Vedas asking for prosperity, success in war or bliss in the hereafter, the portion of the Atharva Veda condemned for its crudeness helps to give us a complete picture of the society of those days. There is no question of the Rig Veda presenting a view of that society in an earlier and purer and the Atharva in a later and more degenerate condition. The one supplements the other. The story of the Gadarene swine cannot be left out of a consideration of the society in which Jesus preached the Sermon on the Mount."

And then he states his considered view:

"My own conviction is that the Atharva Veda contains Suktas pregnant with a spiritual meaning and containing the highest teachings on Yoga and Vedanta, whose proportion is quite as high as that of similar pieces in the Rig Veda. European scholars, obsessed by the idea that the old Aryan religion was, at the best, a higher form of animism and nature-worship, are apt to class all such spiritual and philosophical discourses as later accretions. I do not accept their premisses and cannot accept their conclusions...

That it was not previously recognised as a Veda even if the Mantras it contains did form one definite collection —a very doubtful proposition, indeed,—is tolerably certain. It is equally certain that it gradually won its way to its present status through its intrinsic merits, the profundity of the thought it embodied, the catholicity of its general approach, the lofty tone of its moral injunctions and the message of help and hope which it brings to the ordinary man and woman who has one eye fixed on heaven but cannot take the other away from the immediate calls of this world.

It should be worthwhile to pursue this matter further and see if the Atharva is not the bearer of a tradition which later developed into the Agama school of thought and worship, culminating in the prolific systems covered by the name Tantra."

And indeed it is so. For, as Sri Aurobindo points out, the course of the religious-spiritual awakening and development in these early societies was closely paralleled by a growth of occult knowledge and practice. Whether in India or Egypt or the other Mediterranean countries, the Mystics who were the leaders of society, not only fathomed the depths of the soul but were equally occupied in discovering the secrets of Nature, in delving into the depths of the mysteries that opened behind and beyond the physical universe. They probed into these secrets and sought to gain control over their powers even as the scientists of today aim at an increasing control over the forces of physical Nature. And it is a fragment of this tradition that is found recorded in the Atharva Veda. The Tantra takes up and carries forward this line of life and thought, harmonises it, as far as possible, with the developments, religious, spiritual and social, that marked the later Indian societies. We do not need to dwell more on this topic at the moment. Suffice to say that far from being a manual of charms and magic, white and black, the Atharva Samhita is a rich souvenir of the spiritual and the occult heritage of ancient India.

The subject-matter of the treatise before us is what is known as the *Vrātya Kāṇḍa* and forms the fifteenth section of the Atharva text (Shaunaka recension)[1]. The Book of Vratya, consisting of 220 prose Mantras whose seer is Atharva and the Deity Vratya, is singular in that no authoritative commentator has dealt with it. Even Sayana, the author observes, passed it by with just a short introductory paragraph. It has been left alone owing to its obscurity. It is however fortunate that the text has found an able and sympathetic commentator in the person of Dr. Sampurnanandji who is known for his erudite scholarship in Sanskrit and Hindi and it is particularly gratifying that an English version of his original commentary in Sanskrit, *S'rutiprabhā*, is now made available so as to reach a wider circle.

[1] It forms part of the eighteenth Kanda of the Paippalada recension.

Now, at the very outset the question arises, who is *Vrātya*? The author points out that normally the word would apply to one who has not been initiated into the Vedic sacraments and hence not competent to participate in its ritual. But also the term came to denote certain tribes, nomadic and backward, who were outside the pale of Aryan society and paid no heed to its ethos. Vratya also applied to the Sannyasin or the recluse who was not a practicant of the Vedic religion and to whom the injunctions of the Veda did not apply. But this is not all. In the Veda the word *Vrātya* signifies the supreme God Himself. For the Paramatman is the Vratya *par excellence*. He is bound by nothing, attached to nothing. He is indeed the base and the continent of all; yet he transcends all; he is the ultimate Vratya.

The text describes the birth of the cosmos out of the conscient Being of Brahman, the Vratya. The Paramatman moves into the poise of the Creator, the Prajapati who beholds 'the gold within himself and gives birth to it', i.e., manifests the Truth-Substance with which he is charged. From this One Substance issues the manifold creation of the Gods, the Powers, the Manes, Men, Plants and Animals—the entire universe governed by His Will and Power.

He who seeks and realises in himself this Knowledge of the Godhead, verily becomes himself a Vratya and functions as a living centre for the radiation of this Truth of Brahman.

The supreme Vratya is himself manifest here as the Virat Purusha and he is to be approached and adored in each of the forms that people this variegated creation.

This in substance is the theme of the book which has been developed in the picturesque language so natural to the fresh, imaginative and symbolic mentality of the Vedic Poet.

The Commentary is lucid, learned and live with the spirit of the Shruti. It is pleasing to note that when called upon by the demands of the text, the author does not hesitate to step beyond the confines of the traditional interpretation[1] though in certain portions one cannot help feeling that the commentator could have pursued, with greater results, the line of spiritual interpretation which is as old as the Veda itself and has been revived and re-stated in recent times by Sri Aurobindo.

Speaking of *Satya* and *Ṛta* born of the Tapas, the writer does not treat them as synonyms as many commentators do. Their distinct connotation and use at the hands of the Vedic seers does not escape his keen mind. He writes: 'Both these words are commonly translated as Truth, in spite of the fact that they are often mentioned together and obviously stand for different concepts. It is true that in common parlance, they do mean truth but in philosophical, specially Vedic literature, they have a different connotation. Rita means the immutable law of nature and Satya the equally inescapable law of morality."

We are afraid the significance of these terms is wider and other. Satyam in the Veda (and the Upanishad) stands not for morality, veracity or any other human standard or law of conduct but for the essential Truth of

---

[1] For instance, commenting on the text: *He became Eka-vratya. He grasped the bow*; *that verily is Indra's bow*, the author leaves the usual meaning of rainbow and observes: "The bow is the supreme power, the aggregate of all powers and forces. Vak says, 'I give the bow to Rudra to destroy the enemies of the Veda with arrows."

existence (*Sat*). There is a Satyam of the infra-human order in creation where the law of morality does not hold good even as there is a Satyam of the supra-human order. There is a truth that bases every form, every being, every existence. Each form, individual or universal, has its Truth, Satya, which it is its business to manifest. This fundamental Truth at the base of every existence is *Satyam* and the Knowledge corresponding to this Truth, the Truth-Consciousness, what Sri Aurobindo calls the ordered truth of active being, is *Ṛtam*.

We are unable to agree that the *gold* which Prajapati saw in himself and gave birth to (XV.I.1.2) refers to 'the sum-total of the residual effects of the virtuous and vicious acts of the jivas during the life-cycles of the preceding universe.' In the Process of manifestation, the jivas and their samskaras, arise much later or farther than the stage at which the Brahman perceives himself as the Hiranyagarbha. He manifests freely out of his own supreme Will. The Brahman is self-poised as the Creator Hiranyagarbha and regards in his own Being the Substance of Truth—the Gold—which seeks to manifest.

OTHER TITLES BY SRI M.P. PANDIT: